Eyewitness
Battle

Dutch wheel-
lock pistol

Indian
spiked mace

British
shoulder scales

French
footsoldier's
backpack

Italian
linstock

British
shoulder
belt plate

Polish or
Hungarian
war hammer

US Gatling gun

Turkish Order
of Osmanieh

Eyewitness
Battle

British
Victoria Cross

Written by
RICHARD HOLMES

Photographed by
GEOFF DANN & GEOFF BRIGHTLING

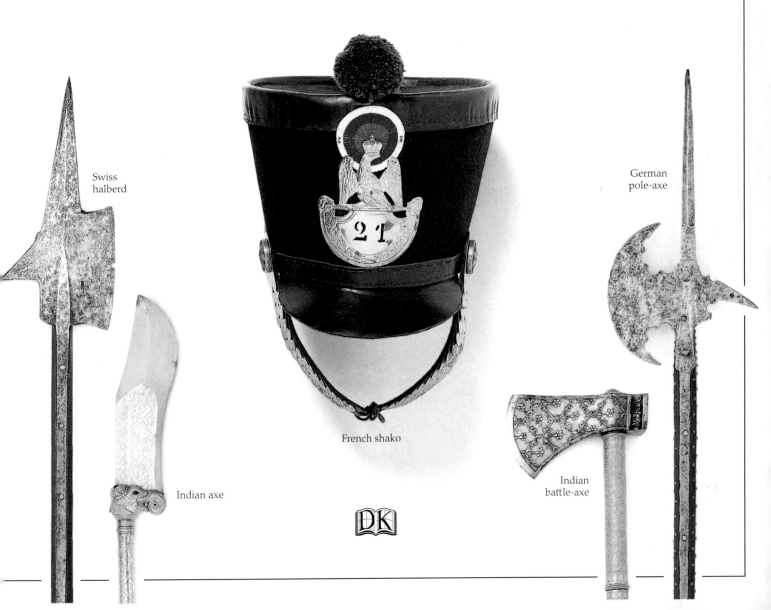

Swiss
halberd

German
pole-axe

French shako

Indian axe

Indian
battle-axe

DK

Caucasian pistol

British commemorative
medal

Model of private
of 71st Highland
Light Infantry

German
swept-hilt
rapier

Indian
battle-axe

British
gorget

Buttons of the 52nd
Oxfordshire Light
Infantry regiment

DK

LONDON, NEW YORK,
MELBOURNE, MUNICH, AND DELHI

Project editor Caroline Beattie
Art editor Sharon Spencer
DTP/Design Ivan Finnegan
Managing editor Gillian Denton
Managing art editor Julia Harris
Researcher Céline Carez
Production Catherine Semark
Picture research Cynthia Hole

REVISED EDITION
Project editors Jayne Miller, Steve Setford
Art editors Edward Kinsey, Peter Radcliffe
Managing editor Camilla Hallinan
Managing art editor Owen Peyton Jones
Art director Martin Wilson
Associate publisher Andrew Macintyre
Production editor Laragh Kedwell
Production controller Pip Tinsley
Picture research Myriam Megharbi

This Eyewitness ® Guide has been conceived by
Dorling Kindersley Limited and Editions Gallimard

First published in Great Britain in 1995
This revised edition published in 2009 by
Dorling Kindersley Limited, 80 Strand, London WC2R ORL

Copyright © 1995, © 2009 Dorling Kindersley Limited
A Penguin Company

2 4 6 8 10 9 7 5 3 1
ED768 – 02/09

A CIP catalogue record for this book is available
from the British Library

ISBN: 978-1-40533-776-2

Colour reproduction by Colourscan, Singapore
Printed by Toppan Co. (Shenzen) Ltd., China

Discover more at
www.dk.com

Contents

Japanese Order
of the Rising Sun

What is battle?

BATTLE IS A CLASH between groups of armed people. It spans most cultures and all continents. Its character – the duration, the number of participants, the weapons, and the tactics employed – is infinitely variable. Battle is intimately bound up with the social, economic, technical, and political features of its age. In the European tradition it was a way for the rulers of one country to force those of another to comply with their wishes. Asian cultures often avoided battle and sought to win by rapid movement or protracted operations. Battle presented many challenges to the courage and resolve of combatants. The German military theorist Carl von Clausewitz (1780–1831) warned that "the character of battle … is slaughter, and its price is blood."

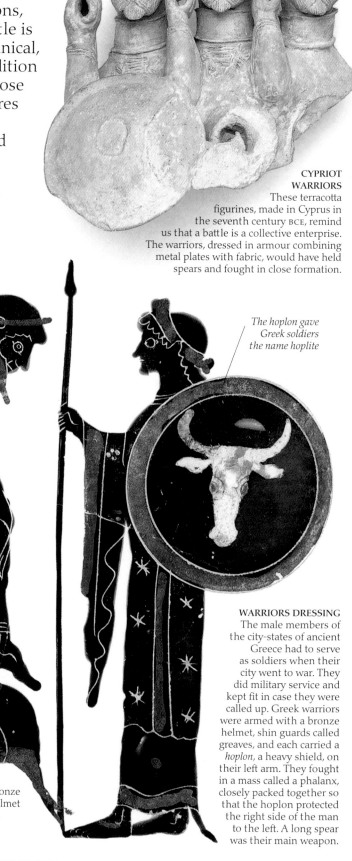

Original statue would have had spear fitted into right hand

CYPRIOT WARRIORS
These terracotta figurines, made in Cyprus in the seventh century BCE, remind us that a battle is a collective enterprise. The warriors, dressed in armour combining metal plates with fabric, would have held spears and fought in close formation.

Spear

The hoplon gave Greek soldiers the name hoplite

Greave being fitted

Bronze helmet

WARRIORS DRESSING
The male members of the city-states of ancient Greece had to serve as soldiers when their city went to war. They did military service and kept fit in case they were called up. Greek warriors were armed with a bronze helmet, shin guards called greaves, and each carried a *hoplon*, a heavy shield, on their left arm. They fought in a mass called a phalanx, closely packed together so that the hoplon protected the right side of the man to the left. A long spear was their main weapon.

FLEEING ARABS

The great battles of history were often short, for the effort of plying a sword or a spear quickly exhausted combatants. Defeated warriors fled, and might escape by throwing away their heavy weapons and equipment. Training and discipline were battle-winners. The Assyrians, who lived in the area of modern Iraq in around 1300–600 BCE, were fierce and well organized; these Arabs are fleeing from them.

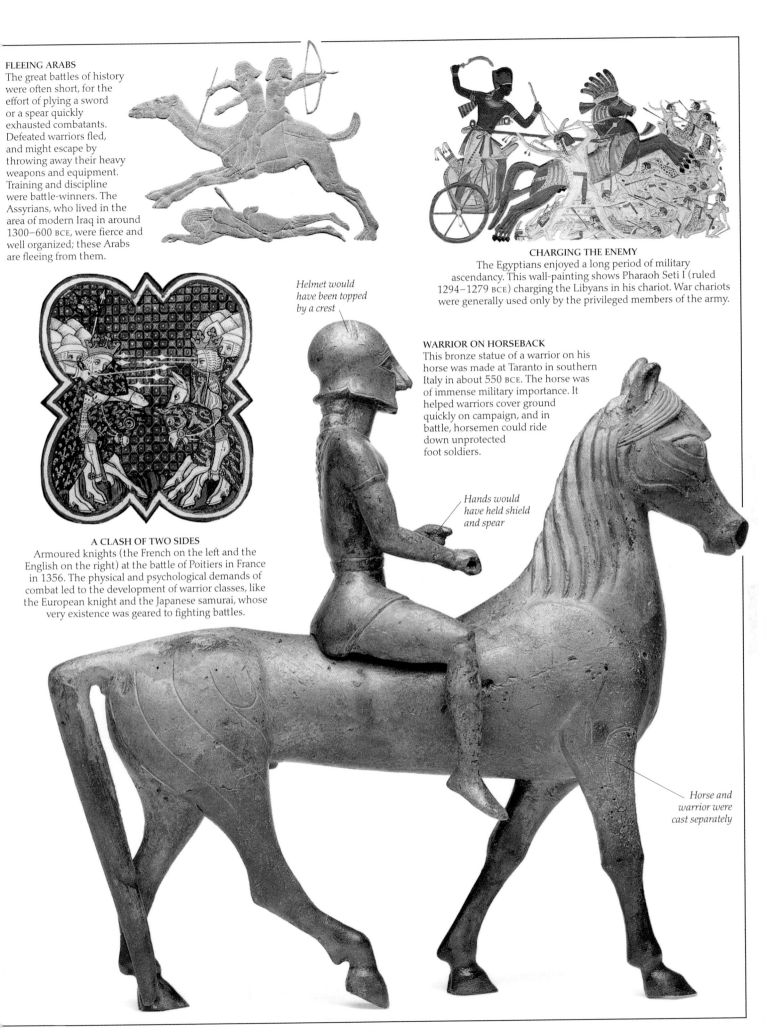

CHARGING THE ENEMY

The Egyptians enjoyed a long period of military ascendancy. This wall-painting shows Pharaoh Seti I (ruled 1294–1279 BCE) charging the Libyans in his chariot. War chariots were generally used only by the privileged members of the army.

Helmet would have been topped by a crest

WARRIOR ON HORSEBACK

This bronze statue of a warrior on his horse was made at Taranto in southern Italy in about 550 BCE. The horse was of immense military importance. It helped warriors cover ground quickly on campaign, and in battle, horsemen could ride down unprotected foot soldiers.

Hands would have held shield and spear

A CLASH OF TWO SIDES

Armoured knights (the French on the left and the English on the right) at the battle of Poitiers in France in 1356. The physical and psychological demands of combat led to the development of warrior classes, like the European knight and the Japanese samurai, whose very existence was geared to fighting battles.

Horse and warrior were cast separately

Infantry of the line

INFANTRY FORMED THE GREAT MASS of most armies, and unskilled recruits who volunteered for or were conscripted into service would usually serve as foot soldiers. In the 18th and 19th centuries, infantry units formed an army's line of battle, so they were called regiments of the line. Regiments were numbered or named after a geographical region; sometimes they were known by the names of their colonels. There were specialist infantry, such as light regiments or rifle regiments, intended for skirmishing, and grenadiers, initially formed to use the hand-grenade but later simply elite foot soldiers.

JOIN UP! JOIN UP!
Although the Pressing Act of 1704 meant that jobless able-bodied men could be drafted into military service, the British army usually relied on volunteers. A drummer would "beat up" to attract them, and a recruiting sergeant or officer would use cash and promises of regular meals and pay to persuade them to enlist.

"I WANT YOU FOR THE US ARMY"
Posters appealed to the patriotic spirit, so as to avoid conscription (forced military service).

TAKING THE KING'S SHILLING
Once a man had accepted money from the recruiting sergeant ("taken the King's shilling") by fair means or foul, he was deemed to have enlisted.

Bayonet

National cockade (coloured ribbon, here imitated in metal)

Shako plate with imperial eagle and regimental number

INFANTRY UNIFORM
This uniform was worn by a corporal of the French 21st Regiment of Infantry in the Napoleonic period. The rank of corporal was indicated by the stripes on the lower sleeve. Infantrymen lived, and often died, on their feet, and so their shoes were heavily studded to help them withstand the rigours of campaigning.

Chevron on upper sleeve awarded for five years' good conduct

Shako

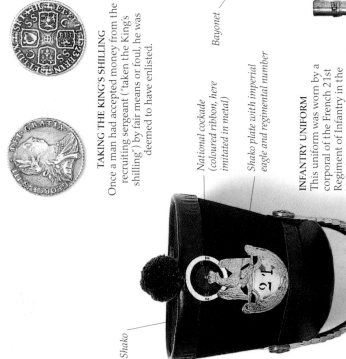

Owner's initials

REPAIR KIT
The hussif (derived from the word housewife) was a case for needles, thread, and other bits of sewing equipment. This example was made from pieces of old uniform and embroidered with the owner's regimental colours (pp. 18–19), those of the 93rd Highlanders. It could be rolled up and put in the pack on the march or hung by the soldier's bedside in camp.

Corporal's stripes

AMMUNITION POUCH
This pouch was worn over the left shoulder on its buff leather strap which incorporated a fitting for the bayonet. It also had a soft cap fastened beneath it.

This 1777-pattern Charleville musket (pp. 42–43) was the most common weapon of the French infantry

Studs helped shoes to last longer

SHORT SWORD
The short sword was carried by most Napoleonic French infantrymen. Its value in combat was limited, but it was put to many other uses, such as chopping wood or holding a kettle over the camp fire, in bivouacs (open-air camps).

DRESSED FOR THE WEATHER
Infantrymen carried warm, long greatcoats which they wore in wet or cold weather. These members of the British 1st Foot Guards are in full marching order (equipment), with packs and cooking utensils on their backs.

FOOT SOLDIERS
Infantrymen fought on foot. Their uniforms served to clothe and protect them from the weather as well as to give each side a distinctive look – the British are in red and the French are in blue.

Brass buckle

PACK
The Napoleonic infantryman's pack was made from the hide of almost any animal that came to hand, and often had the fur left on to make it more hard-wearing. It contained spare clothing and personal effects, and items like a greatcoat or spare shoes could be strapped to the outside.

Loose-fitting trousers were worn for battle over close-fitting knee breeches

Brass buttons embossed with "21", the regimental number

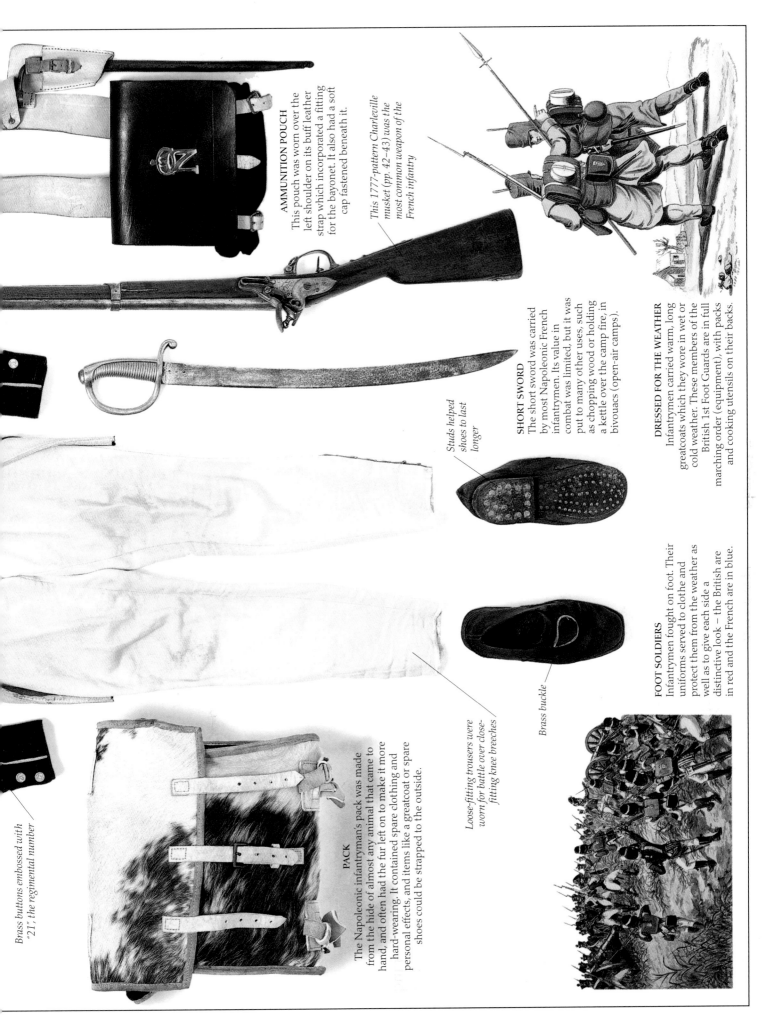

Heavy cavalry

FOR MUCH OF HISTORY, cavalry formed two main groups: light cavalry, whose chief tasks were screening (counter-reconnaissance), scouting, and the pursuit of a beaten enemy; and heavy cavalry, who were used for shock action (the physical impact of horses and people) on the field of battle. Heavy cavalry, who traced their function back to knights, were trained and equipped for the knee-to-knee charge, in which cavalry charged in solid lines. Heavy cavalry were used against both cavalry and infantry. Although it was difficult for even the best cavalry to ride down infantry who stood steady against the onslaught, the thunderous onrush of big men on big horses was very effective, and often persuaded shaky infantry to run. Cuirassiers were the classic type of heavy cavalry, whose prestige helped ensure their survival into the early 20th century. A third category of cavalry, dragoons, began as foot soldiers on horseback; they did most of their fighting dismounted, but were eventually regarded as true cavalry.

CHARGE!
French cuirassiers charge the Germans in the Franco-Prussian War of 1870–1871. The cuirass alone could weigh as much as 5.5–6.8 kg (12–15 lb).

Snaffle bit

Curb bit

BIT BETWEEN THE TEETH
Battles were terrifying both for people and horses, and the simple snaffle bit rarely gave a rider suffcient control of his mount. A harsher curb bit, used with double reins, gave the rider more control.

VALISE
A horseman had to carry an assortment of spare clothing and equipment. This valise, its ends decorated with the number of the horseman's regiment, was attached behind the saddle.

Stirrups

Buckle to attach saddlecloth to saddle

CARBINE
In 1811, French cuirassiers were issued with carbines. These were shorter than the infantry musket so as to be more handy on horseback, although in practice they were more useful for sentries and outposts than on the battlefield.

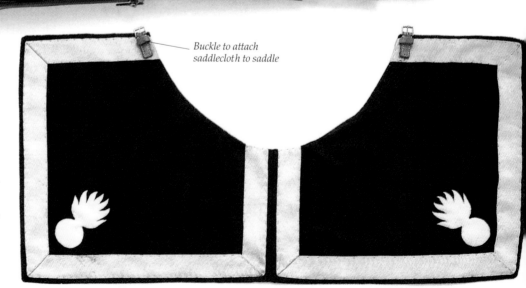

SADDLECLOTH
This saddlecloth was fitted over the horse's hindquarters behind the saddle and under the valise. The grenade badges at its corners symbolize the elite nature of cuirassier regiments. The badge originated with grenadiers, traditionally the biggest and bravest of the infantry, who were trained to throw hand-grenades, but it later denoted select troops in general.

CUIRASS
The steel of this Napoleonic French cuirassier's breastplate was strong enough to keep out musket balls and sword cuts. It was worn over the uniform jacket, and held in place by the shoulder straps and a belt around the waist. The quilted lining protected the wearer from the edges of the metal.

Backplate

Leather shoulder strap, with brass protection

Quilted lining

TUNIC AND TROUSERS
The tunic was made of closely woven material which kept the cold and rain out. The trousers were made of soft white hide, which was comfortable and hard-wearing.

Heavy steel, proof against musket balls

Breast plate

Cuffs decorated with regimental facing colours

Cartridge box for ammunition

BOOTS
Heavy leather boots gave some protection against the jostling that went on as men were pressed together in solid lines.

Feather plume for special occasions

Horsehair tuft

Fur turban

HELMET
A man's head presented a vulnerable target. His elaborate helmet had a steel skull, decorated with a fur turban. An embossed brass comb rose above it, with a long horsehair tail falling to the back, partly as ornament and partly to protect his neck. A small horsehair tuft decorated the front of the helmet. The red feather side-plume was initially worn all the time, but in 1808 the 8th Regiment lost 85 in a single day, so plumes were thereafter worn only on special occasions.

Leather chin strap protected by brass scales

Horsehair "mane"

Epaulettes

Sword-knot worn round the wrist to keep the sword safe

Brass-hilted sword with a straight, heavy blade; cuirassiers were trained to use the point wherever possible

FIGHTING WOMEN
FIGHTING WOMEN
Although women were usually discouraged from taking part in combat, a national emergency often broke down taboos. These Serbian women were taught how to use rifles during a period of unrest in the Balkans.

Weapon training

T HE BATTLEFIELD was a terrifying and deadly place. Soldiers had to balance a natural tendency to run away with the desire not to let down comrades and leaders. Soldiers were drilled to make them use their weapons efficiently, and to create a cohesive fighting unit with the discipline to withstand the shock of battle. Sometimes courage was promoted by a code of values which dominated an entire social class, like knights in medieval Europe or samurai in feudal Japan. Even so, members of a warrior class still needed training to form efficient armies rather than a collection of individual warriors.

Stringed bugle badge

Plume worn by officers, sergeants, and buglers

Cross-belt with whistle for giving orders

Sergeant's chevrons

Backsight: rifles had proper sights, which helped the rifleman aim

Officer's sash

READY, AIM, FIRE!
Some experienced soldiers argued that the aim of drill was to produce unquestioning obedience. Frederick the Great (1713–1786) of Prussia declared that "the common soldier must fear his officer more than the enemy". Others believed in a system founded on two-way trust and respect between officers and men. The British army's rifle regiments obeyed a philosophy that emphasized that "a Corps of Riflemen is expected to be one where intelligence is to distinguish every individual".

Hilt of sword bayonet

Cartridge box contains ammunition

Hessian boots (p. 17) worn with spurs by captains and ranks above (these were mounted, even in infantry regiments)

Waxed canvas gaiters protect feet in wet weather

British riflemen demonstrate five different positions for firing the Baker rifle (pp. 42–43)

HARDEE'S TACTICS

Drill-books were written by officers who hoped to make money or enhance their reputations. These books became especially important when small armies grew rapidly and there were too few trained instructors. Hardee's *Tactics* was widely used by the largely amateur officers during the US Civil War (1861–1865).

RIFLE DRILL

Drill-books contained plates of soldiers carrying out the various parts of each drill movement. *The Rifle Manual and Firing Positions* (1804) shows how to "trail arms". In the first part (left) the left hand was brought across the body to seize the rifle level with the shoulder. In the second (centre) the right hand moved up to hold the rifle near its point of balance, and in the third (right) the left hand was removed, allowing the rifle to trail on the right side at arm's length.

SWORD EXERCISES

It was harder to train a cavalryman than an infantryman, for the former had to be able to ride and look after his horse as well as use his weapons. Cavalrymen, like these troopers, were taught sword drill, which consisted of a number of cuts, points (stabbing movements), and parries (blocking an opponent's sword cuts).

British rifle regiments wore green rather than the red of the line infantry

Sling enabled rifle to be carried over shoulder on march

The sitting position was sometimes assumed on hillsides

Soldiers were taught to march in formation

13

Continued on next page

Drill and discipline

Efficient fire and movement depended on slick individual and collective drill. Loading and firing drills were especially important, for they could enable one side to fire faster than the other. In the Napoleonic period well-drilled British infantry were able to fire faster than their opponents. Good drill also helped to avoid accidents: Marshal Gouvion St-Cyr (1764–1830) reckoned that one quarter of French infantry casualties in the Napoleonic period were caused by soldiers being accidentally shot by men behind. Drill, and emphasis on smartness and cleanliness, also helped to create a climate of disciplined obedience, in which the soldier would carry out orders instinctively. Finally, snappy drill and smart uniforms fostered a soldier's self-esteem, giving him pride and confidence in himself and his unit.

MIGHTY RULER
Genghis Khan (1162–1227) led Mongol armies over huge tracts of Central Asia, China, and Russia. He was a skilled general and administrator, and his armies were not the undisciplined hordes of popular mythology, but well-organized bands of horsemen.

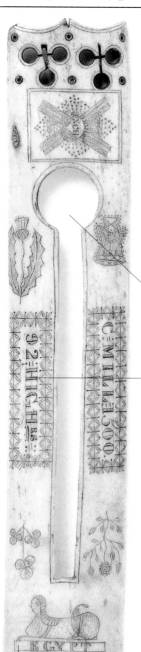

Hole for buttons

Name of owner's regiment

Regimental battle honour for the 1801 Egyptian campaign

Button of 52nd Oxfordshire Regiment (Light Infantry)

BRIGHT AS A BUTTON
In peacetime, much time was devoted to keeping uniform and equipment clean and smart. Brass buttons had to be polished daily, and to avoid the polish staining the tunic, the soldier used a button stick. The buttons were inserted through the hole and then slid down the slot so that several could be polished at once.

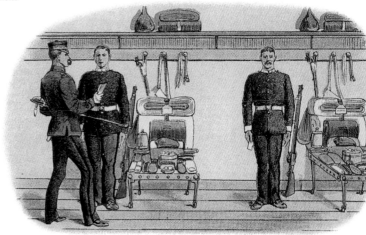

KIT INSPECTION
This scene in a British 19th-century barrack-room would have been familiar to soldiers in most armies. Soldiers laid all their belongings out in a set manner ready for inspection. The officer would check that all items were present, clean, and in good condition.

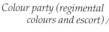

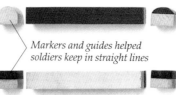

Markers and guides helped soldiers keep in straight lines

Colour party (regimental colours and escort)

Lieutenant-colonel (commanding officer)

Sergeant major

Junior major commands left wing of battalion

Adjutant (commanding officer's personal staff officer)

DRILL BLOCKS
Officers needed to know how to drill large bodies of men so that they could move companies (about 100 men) and battalions (about 800 men) from the column of march to the line of battle and not get them tangled up ("clubbed"). These military drill blocks, each of which represents an individual or a small group of men, enabled officers to practise drawing up units in various formations.

FORMING A SQUARE
There were times when drill was a matter of life and death. Infantrymen in a line were able to deliver the maximum volume of fire, but they were vulnerable to attack by charging cavalry. To meet this threat they formed squares, which were almost invulnerable to cavalry. The drill for forming a square had to be carried out quickly and without fuss.

ADVANCING IN A LINE
These soldiers were trained to march in a straight line in order to use their weapons effectively. They gained reassurance from the presence of comrades to left and right, and brave leadership by officers. The Scots Fusilier Guards (as they were then known) advancing towards the Russians at the Battle of the Alma (Crimean War, 1854–1856).

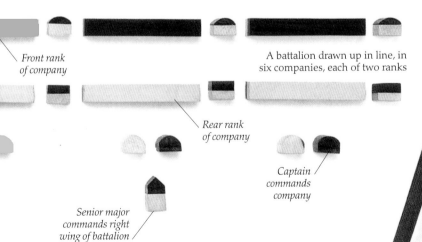

Front rank of company

A battalion drawn up in line, in six companies, each of two ranks

Rear rank of company

Captain commands company

Senior major commands right wing of battalion

Hinge, held by sergeant or sergeant major when stick was in use

Brass bar for adjusting size of pace

PACING IT OUT
To ensure that soldiers moved at the same speed, they were trained to take paces of uniform length, and to take a set number of paces a minute. This pace-stick, really a giant pair of dividers, is still used in the British army for measuring the length of paces.

Polished wood

End tipped with brass to make it more hard-wearing

Badges of rank

Shoulder cord worn by a field-marshal

ZULU ARMY
In the Zulu army, officers were distinguished by leopard-skin kilts or capes and by certain types of blue feather. Although in the 18th century regiments were uniformly dressed, by the end of the 19th century members of inexperienced regiments carried black shields which they exchanged for white ones as their regiment's reputation grew.

ARMIES ARE LARGE and complex organizations, and can only be run efficiently if they have a clear chain of command. Badges of rank enabled status to be recognized easily. They also helped to reinforce the military spirit by creating a climate of discipline and formality. There were many ways of indicating rank, such as the carrying of specific weapons or the wearing of more elaborate clothing by senior personnel. In the Chinese army, for example, the senior mandarins wore tunics embroidered with particular symbols to denote their rank. Gradually, in the 19th century, most armies around the world turned to indicating rank by distinctive badges worn on the sleeve, collar, or epaulette.

Shoulder cord worn by a colonel

Shoulder cord worn by a captain

Badge of a warrant officer class 1, worn on cuff

Parchment leaf

JAPANESE FAN
The war fan was carried by Japanese officers in the time of the samurai as a mark of their rank. It could be used for signalling and, when closed, could parry a sword cut or club an opponent. The fan itself was usually made of iron covered with parchment decorated with the sun of Japan.

Iron sticks

BRITISH BADGES
Most armies make a distinction between commissioned officers, who hold a commission signed by the head of state or commander-in-chief; warrant officers, whose warrant of appointment carries a more junior status; and non-commissioned officers (NCOs), who can be appointed more easily. Over the past century, badges of rank worn on field uniforms have become increasingly inconspicuous to prevent leaders from being singled out by enemy marksmen.

NCO's chevrons (sergeant), worn on sleeve

THE THIN RED LINE
During the Crimean War battle of Balaclava (1854), Russian cavalry threatened the British base in Balaclava itself. The attack was thwarted by the "Thin Red Line" of the 93rd Sutherland Highlanders. The officer directing the fire shows his rank by wearing a sash and epaulettes and by carrying a sword. There is a corporal, with two chevrons, in the front rank, and a sergeant, with three chevrons, to the rear.

NCO's chevrons (corporal), worn on sleeve

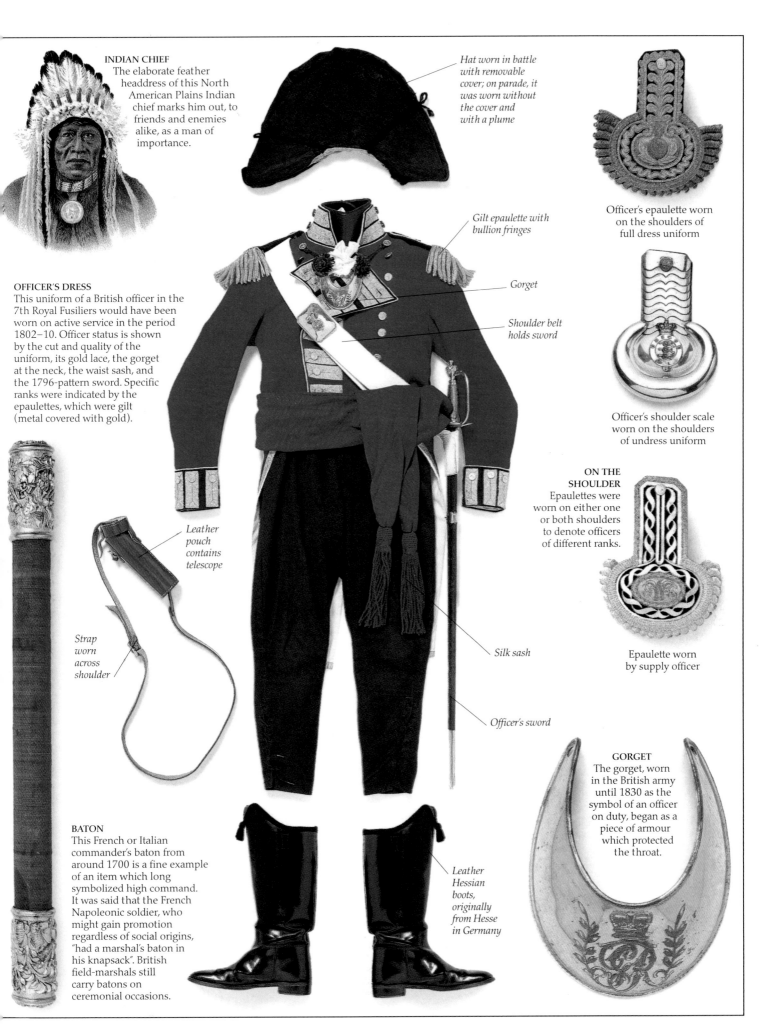

INDIAN CHIEF
The elaborate feather headdress of this North American Plains Indian chief marks him out, to friends and enemies alike, as a man of importance.

Hat worn in battle with removable cover; on parade, it was worn without the cover and with a plume

Officer's epaulette worn on the shoulders of full dress uniform

Gilt epaulette with bullion fringes

Gorget

Shoulder belt holds sword

Officer's shoulder scale worn on the shoulders of undress uniform

OFFICER'S DRESS
This uniform of a British officer in the 7th Royal Fusiliers would have been worn on active service in the period 1802–10. Officer status is shown by the cut and quality of the uniform, its gold lace, the gorget at the neck, the waist sash, and the 1796-pattern sword. Specific ranks were indicated by the epaulettes, which were gilt (metal covered with gold).

ON THE SHOULDER
Epaulettes were worn on either one or both shoulders to denote officers of different ranks.

Leather pouch contains telescope

Strap worn across shoulder

Epaulette worn by supply officer

Silk sash

Officer's sword

BATON
This French or Italian commander's baton from around 1700 is a fine example of an item which long symbolized high command. It was said that the French Napoleonic soldier, who might gain promotion regardless of social origins, "had a marshal's baton in his knapsack". British field-marshals still carry batons on ceremonial occasions.

Leather Hessian boots, originally from Hesse in Germany

GORGET
The gorget, worn in the British army until 1830 as the symbol of an officer on duty, began as a piece of armour which protected the throat.

Regimental colours

Like the eagles carried by Roman legions and the banners of medieval nobles, colours had both symbolic and practical importance. Symbolically, colours were the soul of a regiment: their loss in battle was a matter of deep disgrace. A British officer, whose regiment was in a desperate plight at Waterloo, felt relieved when he saw the "dear old rags" marched off to safety. Practically, they enabled soldiers to recognize their units and rally to them in the confusion of battle. The colour was regularly trooped through the ranks of a regiment so that men would recognize it.

COATS OF ARMS
Early colours often had items from the commanding officer's coat of arms. This shield, carried by King Matthias Corvinus of Hungary and Bohemia (around 1443–1490), bears his arms.

BATTLE HONOURS
Glorious past achievements were marked in many ways. This British shabraque (officer's horse-blanket) is embroidered with battle honours for Dettingen (1743), the Peninsular War (1808–1814), Waterloo (1815), Egypt (1882), and Tel el Kebir (1882).

Silk matches facings (collars and cuffs) on uniforms

Colours normally supported in this belt

COLOUR PARTY
The regimental colour of the 9th East Norfolk Regiment is carried by an ensign, the most junior rank of commissioned officer, whose title is itself another word for flag. Behind him a colour sergeant uses his short pike to defend the colour. Ensigns were usually very young, and in close-quarter battle relied heavily on their colour sergeants to defend them.

HUSSAR STANDARD
French hussar standard, from the time of the republic in the late 18th century. This republican pattern was replaced by one with Napoleonic eagles. Hussars and other light cavalry, whose tasks demanded risk and isolation, did not always carry standards.

CHINESE COLOURS
Here a Japanese officer is in the act of capturing a Chinese flag in the Sino-Japanese war over Korea (1894–1895). The symbolism of colours was international.

BEISSANCE

A LA LOI.

...LENTIA

HUSSARDS

Number indicates 7th Hussars

Symbol of unity

Eagle held thunderbolt as a symbol of power

EAGLE
The Emperor Napoleon introduced the eagle as France's national symbol, and the eagles carried by French regiments consciously harked back to those of the Roman legions. This eagle of the French 105th Regiment of the Line was lost to the British at Waterloo in 1815.

FIGHT FOR THE STANDARD
Regimental colours inevitably became the centre of fierce fighting as attackers sought to seize them from their bearers. Here Union and Confederate cavalrymen struggle for possession of a Confederate standard during the US Civil War (1861–1865). Men often risked their lives to protect their colours: at the Battle of Rezonville (Franco-Prussian War, 1870–1871), the colours of the French 3rd Grenadiers of the Guard were passed from hand to hand as successive bearers were shot down. Eventually the regimental commander died waving them and shouting "To the colour, my boys".

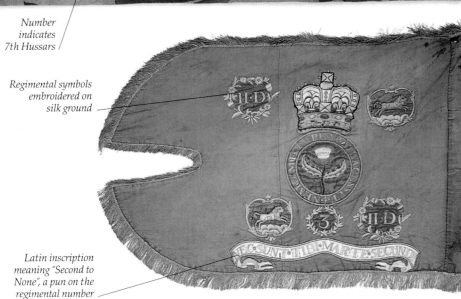

Regimental symbols embroidered on silk ground

Latin inscription meaning "Second to None", a pun on the regimental number

CAVALRY COLOURS
Guidon of the 3rd Troop, 2nd Royal North British Dragoons, about 1780. This swallow-tailed guidon is typical of cavalry standards. For many years colours were carried by individual infantry companies or cavalry troops, but the practice generally died out in the 18th century.

Supply and transport

INDIAN CAVALRY
Asian commanders, facing inhospitable terrain, and distances which dwarfed those in Europe, needed a firm grasp on logistics. The horse armies of antiquity – like the Magyars of Hungary, the Seljuk Turks, and the Mongols – were masters of rapid movement. These 18th-century cavalrymen from the northwest Indian state of Jaipur have bags of provisions hanging from their camels.

LOGISTICS IS THE PRACTICAL ART of moving an army and keeping it supplied: there is much truth in the saying that "Amateurs talk tactics while professionals talk logistics". Until World War I, food for men and horses was an army's main requirements. Many commanders tried to "live off the country" by obtaining food from areas they crossed. But even the small armies of medieval Europe (some as small as 8,000 men) found this difficult. Armies also needed large numbers of horses. In 1700 an army of 60,000 men would have had about 40,000 horses. These would eat 508 tonnes (500 tons) of fodder a day. Inventions like the steam train, motor lorry, and tinned food made things simpler, but at the same time improvements in weaponry increased the burden: by 1916 a British infantry division needed 20 railway wagons of food and 30 of ammunition every day.

FRENCH TROOPS ENTRAINING
The railway revolutionized war, enabling huge armies to be moved quickly and in a more organized way, with fewer accidents or desertions. In addition, soldiers and horses would be rested and fit to fight on arrival at the battlefield. In the Austro-Prussian War of 1866, the Prussians sent 200,000 men to the frontier with astonishing speed. In World War I (1914–1918), so many of the Frenchmen who went to war by train in 1914 did not return that it was said that they had been "eaten by the Gare de l'Est" (a large station in Paris).

SOYER COOKER
British army food was almost inedible during the Crimean War (1853–1856). The great chef Alexis Soyer (1809–1858) went out to help improve cooking. Here he is shown (on the left of the central group) with one of his specially designed cookers behind him.

THE RUSSIAN RAILWAY
The railway was very valuable to large nations, or ones that, like Germany in World War I, had to face enemies on two sides. These Cossacks are being transported eastwards on the Trans-Siberian Railway to reinforce the Russian army fighting the Japanese in Manchuria during the Russo-Japanese War of 1904–1905.

Saxon baggage wagon, used to transport provisions or camping equipment

Pair of horses attached here

TRAVELLING FORGE
Horses required new horseshoes at regular intervals: in August 1914 one of the five German armies in France had 84,000 horses. This travelling forge was kept going on the line of march, enabling blacksmiths to shoe horses or repair metalwork.

Part attached to horse

Bellows to fan fire

Coals kept hot by being blown by bellows

BIVOUAC IN SPAIN
Moving armies could either be billeted (lodged with local inhabitants) or could bivouac, or camp, in improvised open-air encampments. Bivouacking was essential in sparsely populated areas, and was a way of keeping men under better control. Here British soldiers are setting up a bivouac in Spain during the Peninsular War (1808–1814).

Lid lifts to give access to baggage

Large wheels were better on poor roads

FRENCH *VIVANDIERE*
Civilian merchants provided armies with many of their needs. French regiments had uniformed *vivandières* to sell comforts like nips of brandy. This cartoon from the Crimean War shows a *vivandière* mocking the Russians.

SAXON BAGGAGE WAGON
Until transport services became organized as a uniformed branch of the army in the 19th century, armies supplemented their own wagons with civilian vehicles and drivers when war broke out. This led to difficulties as drivers deserted and wagons broke down. Wagons built for military purposes were robust; this one was also small enough to be moved by soldiers if necessary. This wagon was used by the Saxon army in the late 18th century.

A soldier's pack

A SOLDIER'S LIFE ON THE ROAD involved weeks, even months of carrying spare clothing, water, cooking equipment, tools, and ammunition. Because stocking up on supplies was not always convenient, each man was responsible for carrying his own things for the duration of a campaign; experienced soldiers tended to jettison non-essential items. Equipment was often designed so that items not required in battle were kept in a backpack which could be removed before action, but this was not ideal because the victor would have to pause to recover his pack and the vanquished might lose his altogether.

Woollen cloak

Pack for personal items and three days' rations

Mattock for digging ditches

Leather bottle for water or wine

Turf cutter for building turf ramparts

Shaft of javelin

ROMAN SOLDIER
A fully loaded legionary marched with a pack on his back in addition to his helmet, armour, shield, and weapons. The burden weighed 40 kg (90 lb) or more, and might have had to be carried up to 32 km (20 miles) a day.

String was doused with water to keep contents cool

A soldier's water bottle, which stayed with him throughout his service

A PACK UNPACKED
Much of what a soldier carried, like spare clothing and cooking utensils, was government issue. A change of clothes called fatigues was included, and they were worn when off-duty and for doing fatigues (chores) such as cleaning the mess. Many personal items, such as a razor and a shaving brush, were bought privately. No seasoned soldier wished to carry more than was necessary, but "home comforts" could make all the difference on campaigns in inhospitable places.

Camp kettle, used as a cooking pot as well as a plate

Bill-hook for cutting food and chopping firewood

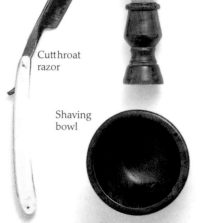

Shoe brush

Badger-hair shaving brush

Fork, knife, and spoon

Cutthroat razor

Shaving bowl

Clothes brush

Soap

Tin mug

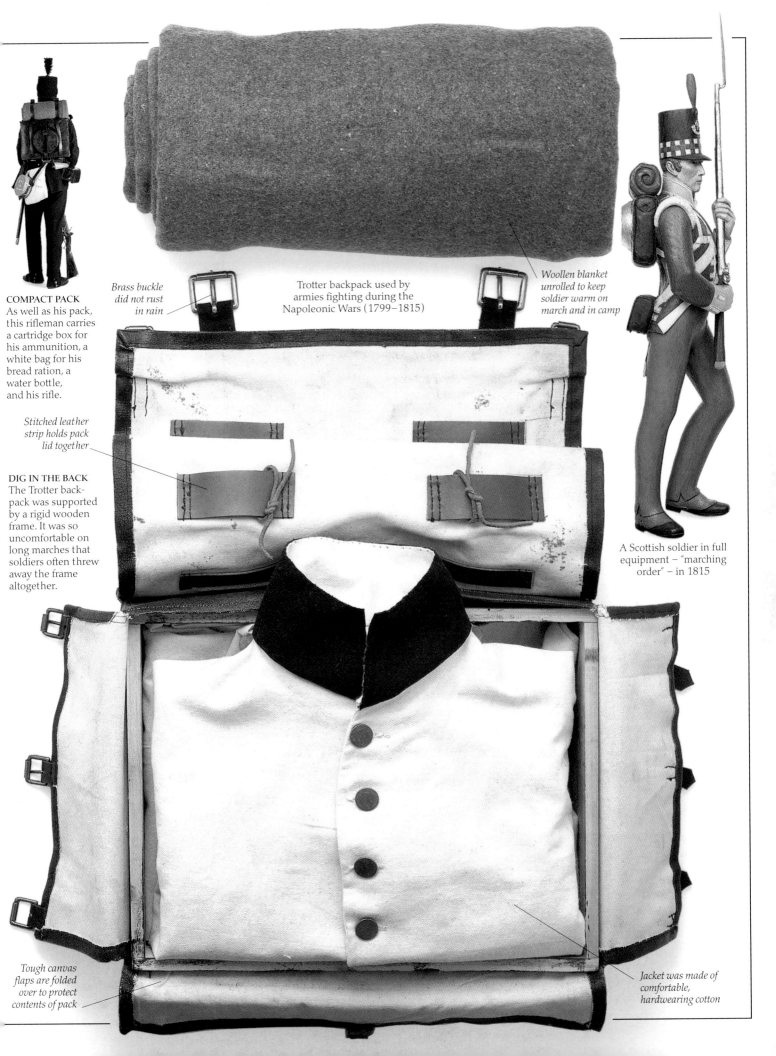

COMPACT PACK
As well as his pack, this rifleman carries a cartridge box for his ammunition, a white bag for his bread ration, a water bottle, and his rifle.

Brass buckle did not rust in rain

Trotter backpack used by armies fighting during the Napoleonic Wars (1799–1815)

Woollen blanket unrolled to keep soldier warm on march and in camp

Stitched leather strip holds pack lid together

DIG IN THE BACK
The Trotter backpack was supported by a rigid wooden frame. It was so uncomfortable on long marches that soldiers often threw away the frame altogether.

A Scottish soldier in full equipment – "marching order" – in 1815

Tough canvas flaps are folded over to protect contents of pack

Jacket was made of comfortable, hardwearing cotton

Reconnaissance

T HE DUKE OF WELLINGTON (1769–1852), a British military commander, declared that the business of war consisted of finding out "what you don't know from what you do". Reconnaissance (surveying an area to gather information) is of fundamental importance, for without it commanders cannot know the strength or location of hostile forces or the nature of the ground they wish to cross. They risk being taken by surprise, or advancing into country where an army will find it hard to move or to sustain itself. For centuries light cavalry, riding well ahead of the advancing columns, was the main means of reconnaissance, although it was also done on foot. With the development first of balloons and then aircraft, the "cavalry of the clouds" assumed growing importance, but even in the 21st century a mix of air and ground reconnaissance works best.

Emblem of French 8th Hussars

SABRETACHE
It is not easy for someone on a horse to keep writing materials accessible yet protected from the weather. So soldiers on reconnaissance, as well as others, wore a sabretache, which was in effect a field writing-case. Inside it were compartments for pens, ink, and writing paper. The outer flap was usually decorated.

Sabretache hung on sword belt

COMPASS
This compass could be used both for verifying the direction of a march and for finding out the geographical location of distant places such as a house or a hill.

Lid to protect inner glass

Glass cover

Needle moves to show North

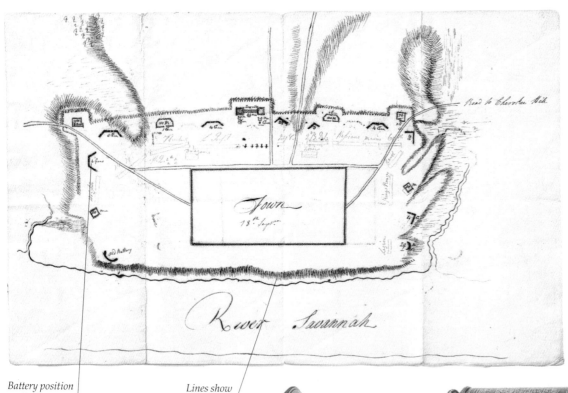

Road to Cherokee Hill

Town 18th Septr

River Savannah

Battery position for four guns

Lines show steep slope

SKETCH
This sketch-map of the fortifications of Savannah, in Georgia (US), was made by a Swiss officer in the British service during the American Revolutionary War (1775–1783). Officers needed to make an accurate record of information they acquired, and field sketching was widely taught at military academies.

TELESCOPE
For centuries commanders used the "perspective glass" (telescope) to observe enemy positions. This is a signaller's telescope, which enabled its user to read flag or light signals in the distance.

Telescope retracts for storage

OBSERVATION BALLOON
On 26 June 1794, a French army met an allied Austro-German army at Fleurus, in Belgium. The French sent up a balloon, named *L'Entreprenant*, to hang over the battlefield, and observers sent messages sliding down its rope. However, these were of little value, and although the French won the battle, observation balloons fell out of favour until the US Civil War (1861–1865).

A view of the Battle of Fleurus painted on the lid of a snuff box

Strap to hang binoculars around neck when in use

RECONNAISSANCE AIRCRAFT
Military aircraft made their debut in 1911 when the Italians flew reconnaissance missions against the Turkish in Tripolitania (in Libya) and dropped some small bombs. Although air reconnaissance provided good information, pilots ran the risk of being shot down once they had been seen.

BROADER VIEW
Originally made from two telescopes joined together, binoculars were easier to use than a telescope. Although they did not usually produce the same degree of magnification, they generally gave a broader field of view. This pair of binoculars was presented by one officer to another officer who had saved his life.

Case to protect lenses when binoculars were not in use

HUSSAR PATROL
These British hussars of 1811 are typical of the light cavalry who played a key role in reconnaissance. They had to move discreetly to avoid being seen or heard by the enemy.

Field guns

FOR MUCH OF HISTORY, cannon were muzzle-loaders (front-loading), firing solid cannonballs at a target well within view. Artillery emerged as the main casualty-producer of 20th-century battles. But this was only after technological advances, mostly in the 19th century, had produced breech-loading (rear-loading) weapons whose explosive shells were more deadly than either the roundshot or primitive shells filled with black powder used by earlier guns.

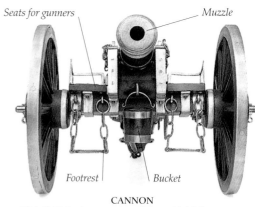

Seats for gunners *Muzzle*

Footrest *Bucket*

CANNON
This British six-pounder of the mid-19th century shows the muzzle-loading cannon at its peak. Its crew of five could fire a 2.7-kg (6-lb) ball to a maximum range of 1,000 m (3,280 feet) two or three times a minute.

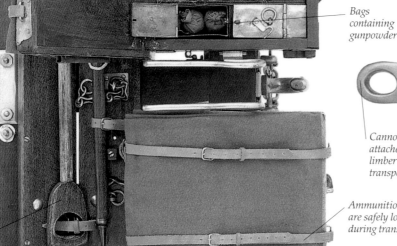

Couplings attached the harnessed horses to the limber

Explosive shells

Fuse to explode shell

Bags containing gunpowder

Tools are stored on the back of the limber

Cannon attached to limber during transport

Ammunition chests are safely locked during transport

LIMBER
The cannon was towed directly behind its limber, whose chest contained sufficient ammunition to keep the gun supplied for some time. Ammunition wagons (caissons) would be used to replenish limbers if ammunition ran short. The limber also carried tools to help the detachment to prepare the gun's position. The six-horse team pulling this gun was attached to the couplings.

ASSEMBLING
When mounting a gun, the barrel required skilled handling. That of a light six-pounder weighed 305 kg (670 lb).

EARLY CANNON
Simple cannon from around 1400 caused few casualties but could terrify both horses and new soldiers.

FUENTES DE ONORO
Horse artillery, with all gunners on horseback, was intended to keep pace with cavalry. At the Battle of Fuentes de Oñoro (Spain, 1811) an English horse artillery battery was surrounded by French cavalry, but the English charged right through the enemy horsemen to escape.

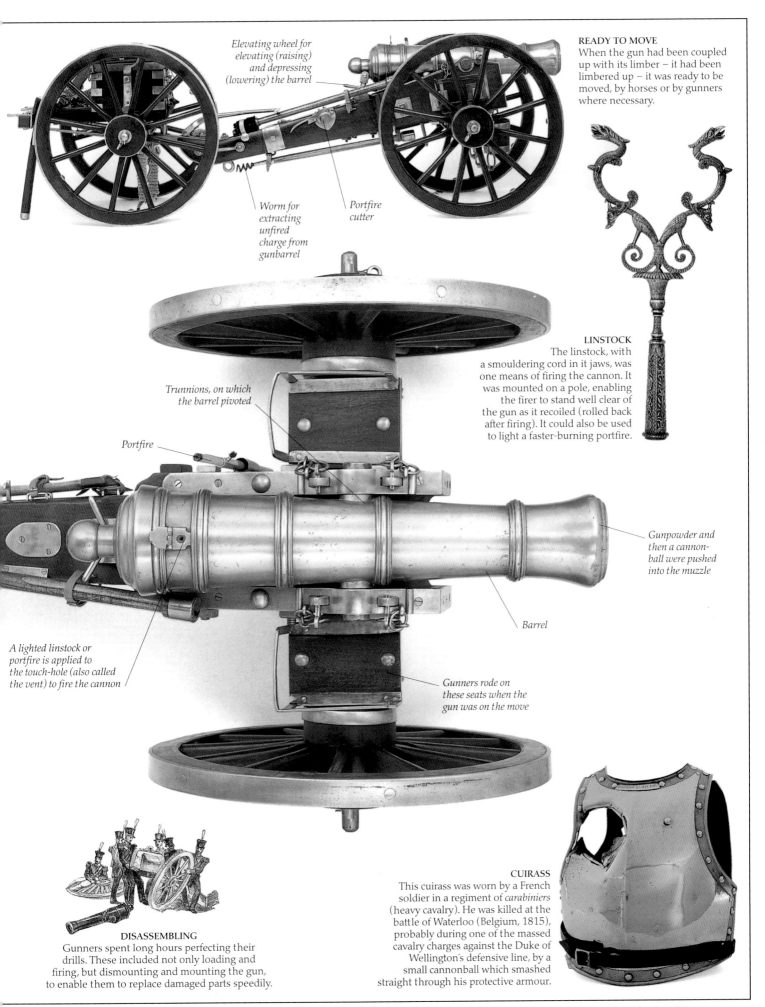

Elevating wheel for elevating (raising) and depressing (lowering) the barrel

Worm for extracting unfired charge from gunbarrel

Portfire cutter

READY TO MOVE
When the gun had been coupled up with its limber – it had been limbered up – it was ready to be moved, by horses or by gunners where necessary.

Trunnions, on which the barrel pivoted

Portfire

LINSTOCK
The linstock, with a smouldering cord in it jaws, was one means of firing the cannon. It was mounted on a pole, enabling the firer to stand well clear of the gun as it recoiled (rolled back after firing). It could also be used to light a faster-burning portfire.

A lighted linstock or portfire is applied to the touch-hole (also called the vent) to fire the cannon

Gunpowder and then a cannon-ball were pushed into the muzzle

Barrel

Gunners rode on these seats when the gun was on the move

DISASSEMBLING
Gunners spent long hours perfecting their drills. These included not only loading and firing, but dismounting and mounting the gun, to enable them to replace damaged parts speedily.

CUIRASS
This cuirass was worn by a French soldier in a regiment of *carabiniers* (heavy cavalry). He was killed at the battle of Waterloo (Belgium, 1815), probably during one of the massed cavalry charges against the Duke of Wellington's defensive line, by a small cannonball which smashed straight through his protective armour.

Continued on next page

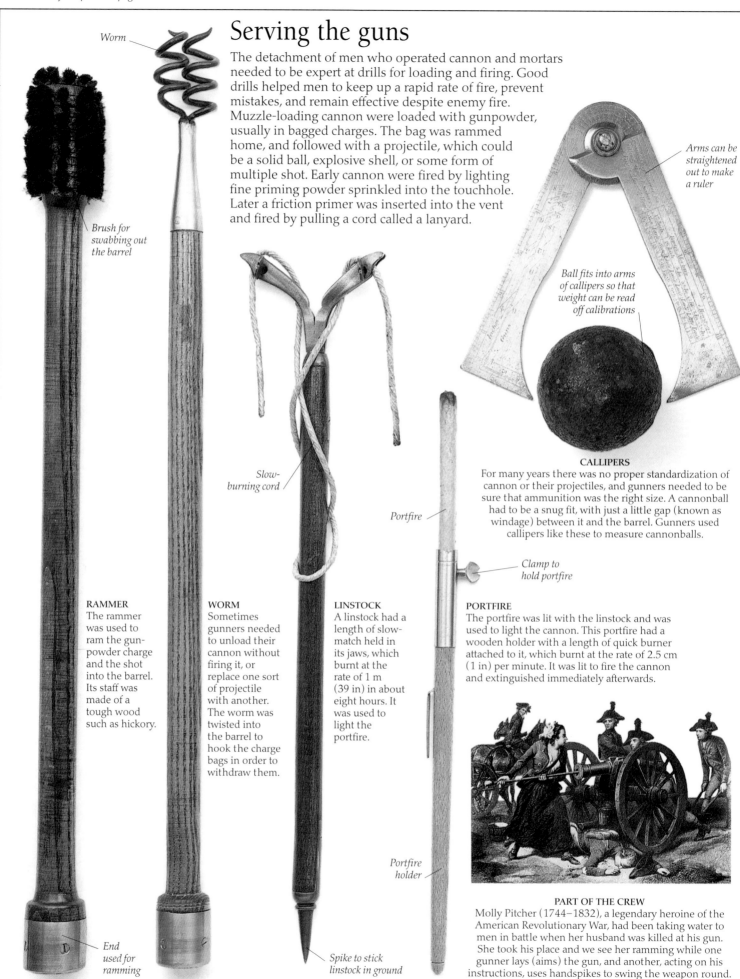

Serving the guns

The detachment of men who operated cannon and mortars needed to be expert at drills for loading and firing. Good drills helped men to keep up a rapid rate of fire, prevent mistakes, and remain effective despite enemy fire. Muzzle-loading cannon were loaded with gunpowder, usually in bagged charges. The bag was rammed home, and followed with a projectile, which could be a solid ball, explosive shell, or some form of multiple shot. Early cannon were fired by lighting fine priming powder sprinkled into the touchhole. Later a friction primer was inserted into the vent and fired by pulling a cord called a lanyard.

Worm

Brush for swabbing out the barrel

Arms can be straightened out to make a ruler

Ball fits into arms of callipers so that weight can be read off calibrations

CALLIPERS
For many years there was no proper standardization of cannon or their projectiles, and gunners needed to be sure that ammunition was the right size. A cannonball had to be a snug fit, with just a little gap (known as windage) between it and the barrel. Gunners used callipers like these to measure cannonballs.

Slow-burning cord

Portfire

Clamp to hold portfire

RAMMER
The rammer was used to ram the gunpowder charge and the shot into the barrel. Its staff was made of a tough wood such as hickory.

WORM
Sometimes gunners needed to unload their cannon without firing it, or replace one sort of projectile with another. The worm was twisted into the barrel to hook the charge bags in order to withdraw them.

LINSTOCK
A linstock had a length of slow-match held in its jaws, which burnt at the rate of 1 m (39 in) in about eight hours. It was used to light the portfire.

PORTFIRE
The portfire was lit with the linstock and was used to light the cannon. This portfire had a wooden holder with a length of quick burner attached to it, which burnt at the rate of 2.5 cm (1 in) per minute. It was lit to fire the cannon and extinguished immediately afterwards.

End used for ramming

Spike to stick linstock in ground

Portfire holder

PART OF THE CREW
Molly Pitcher (1744–1832), a legendary heroine of the American Revolutionary War, had been taking water to men in battle when her husband was killed at his gun. She took his place and we see her ramming while one gunner lays (aims) the gun, and another, acting on his instructions, uses handspikes to swing the weapon round.

FLAMING SHOT
Although solid shot was most common, other projectiles were available. This experimental roundshot was intended to have inflammable material in it to set fire to buildings, for example.

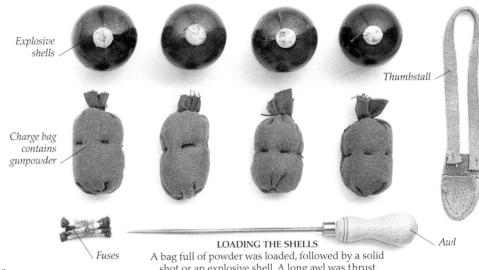

Explosive shells

Charge bag contains gunpowder

Thumbstall

Fuses

Awl

GRAPESHOT
Multiple shot, such as grapeshot, shown here, or canister (a container of musket balls), split up on leaving the gun's muzzle. It was murderous at close range.

LOADING THE SHELLS
A bag full of powder was loaded, followed by a solid shot or an explosive shell. A long awl was thrust through the vent to enable a fuse or fine priming powder to enter the bagged charge. The thumbstall was held over the vent when a gun was swabbed out after firing, to prevent a draught which might light smouldering debris left by the charge bag.

TAKE YOUR PICK
An assortment of tools was carried, usually on the cannon's limber. The pick enabled gunners to break up the ground when they needed to.

THE LAST CANNON
British gunners are here shown firing one of the last muzzle-loading cannon in British service. Breech-loading cannon were successfully used by the Germans in the Franco-Prussian War (1870–1871), and most other nations soon introduced them. The gunners stood clear to avoid injury when the gun jumped back on recoil.

SHOVEL
If gunners had time, they could make their task easier by sloping the earth beneath the gun so that it would naturally roll back into the firing position after recoil.

ESSENTIAL AXE
The axe enabled gunners to cut away roots or branches in the way.

BUCKET FOR THE BARREL
Water was essential for loading, as gunners needed to swab the barrel after firing to ensure that no sparks remained to ignite the next powder charge inserted, and to help remove fouling (the remnants of burnt powder).

Rapid-fire weapons

Traditional weapons had to be laboriously loaded each time they were fired, so inventors experimented with multi-barrelled guns to increase the rate of fire. However, it was not until the mid-19th century that good rapid-fire weapons were produced. The Gatling gun, patented by Dr Richard Gatling (1818–1903), had a number of barrels, most often 10. As they were cranked round by hand, each was fed with a cartridge and fired. A few Gatling guns saw service in the US Civil War (1861–1865) but the weapon was used throughout the world by the 1870s. The French army adopted the mitrailleuse in 1865. Its barrels remained stationary. A plate filled with ammunition was inserted into the breech, and the operator turned the firing crank to fire each barrel in turn.

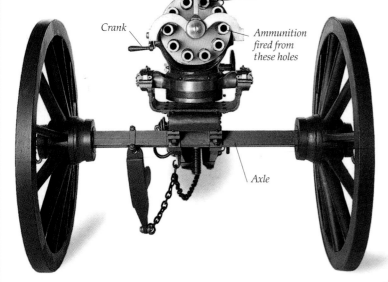

MITRAILLEUSE
The mitrailleuse, whose name literally means "grapeshot shooter", had a maximum effective range of 1,500 m (1,640 yd) against a large target. A gunner inserts a loaded plate.

AMMUNITION
The development of cartridges whose gunpowder was contained in sturdy brass or copper cases made possible the development of rapid-fire weapons. Both the mitrailleuse and the Gatling gun could fire special cartridges containing several bullets. Shown above is a buckshot round for the Gatling.

Crank to turn barrels

Magazine contained cartridges and fed them into the barrel as they were needed

Barrel

Crank

Ammunition fired from these holes

Elevating gear for elevating (raising) and depressing (lowering) the barrels

THE GATLING GUN
Early machine guns were mounted on carriages like conventional field guns. This encouraged officers to regard them as a type of artillery, or to consider them as special weapons for the defence of streets or bridges, because they were heavy and difficult to move. It was not until they were lighter and mounted on tripods (bottom right) that their real potential as infantry weapons emerged.

Axle

Ring to take handspike to swing gun left and right

Trail enabled the gun to be towed and provided a prop when it was in use

Magazine with ammunition; this version of the Gatling, used by the British in India and Africa, took 1-in- (2.5-cm-) calibre cartridges

FRANCO-PRUSSIAN WAR
In the Franco-Prussian War of 1870–1871 the French failed to use the mitrailleuse to best effect, keeping it back with the field guns, rather than pushing it forwards with the infantry. As a consequence it was usually knocked out by superior German cannon. Because development had been secret, few officers and men knew how it worked, and its mechanism was so fragile that untrained men often broke it.

Foresight

Pivot for revolving mechanism

Barrels

THE BUSINESS END
Gatling guns were made in several calibres between 1 cm (.45 in) and 2.5 cm (1 in). Most had ten barrels, which could be cranked fast enough to fire more than 1,000 rounds a minute.

The American, Dr Gatling, in 1893 with his light gun equipped with a drum magazine

Shackle for attaching rope helped gunners move gun on difficult ground

High-angle fire

A CANNON REACHES MAXIMUM RANGE with its barrel at an angle of 45 degrees. Above this level the weapon is said to be firing at a high angle; low-angle fire is below 45 degrees. Mortars were short and stubby, and were specifically designed for high-angle fire. They fired bombs (explosive shells) when most guns fired only solid balls, and they were used in sieges because their projectiles would pass over fortifications to burst inside the town or fortress. Howitzers were longer-barrelled and could fire at low or high angles. Like mortars, they used shells when these were uncommon in cannon. Mortars and howitzers remained important because they could fire over ridges and drop shells into sheltered ground or trench systems. Small "trench mortars" were widely used in World War I (1914–1918).

FIRING UP
The gunner fires an explosive bomb from his mortar over fortifications. Cannon and mortars between them caused a revolution in fortress design. The high stone walls which had characterized medieval fortification offered easy targets. They were replaced by low, squat "artillery fortifications" which were much harder to damage. Important buildings, like powder magazines, were built with strong roofs covered with earth to make them bomb-proof – able to resist mortar bombs.

LOW-ANGLE FIRE
This gunner is using low-angle fire, sending a solid cannonball against fortifications or troops. His cannon is protected by gabions (wicker baskets filled with earth).

GUNNER LIGHTING FUSE
Early mortars required "double ignition". The gunner would first light the fuse on the bomb, and then fire the mortar. This was a dangerous practice: sometimes the mortar failed to fire and its bomb exploded in the barrel, causing casualties and damage. It was later discovered that the flash of the mortar being fired would also ignite the fuse on the bomb.

COEHOORN MORTAR
Not all mortars were heavy. The engineer Menno van Coehoorn (1641–1704), known as "The Dutch Vauban" (pp. 54–55), designed a light mortar which could be manhandled around fortifications or even taken into the field. The Coehoorn mortar was used by many armies, and remained in service until the end of the US Civil War (1861–1865).

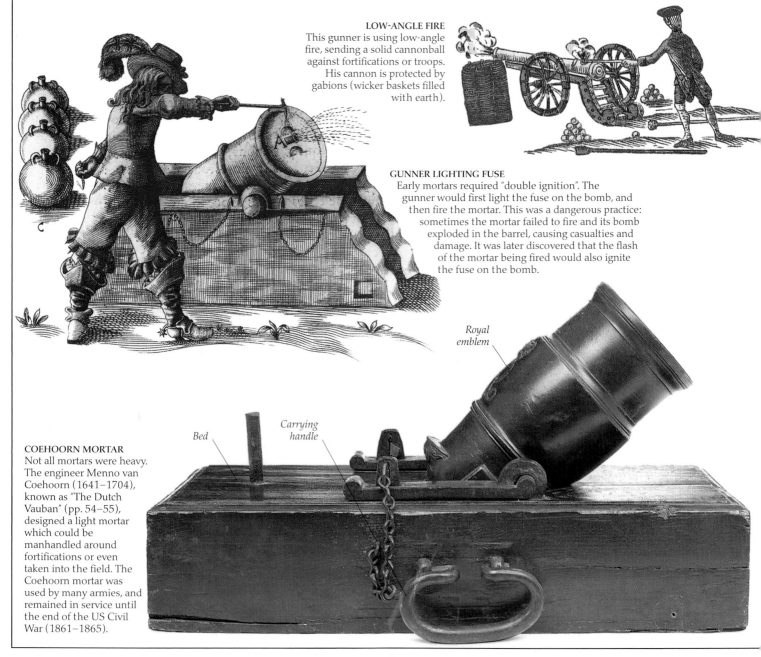

Royal emblem

Bed

Carrying handle

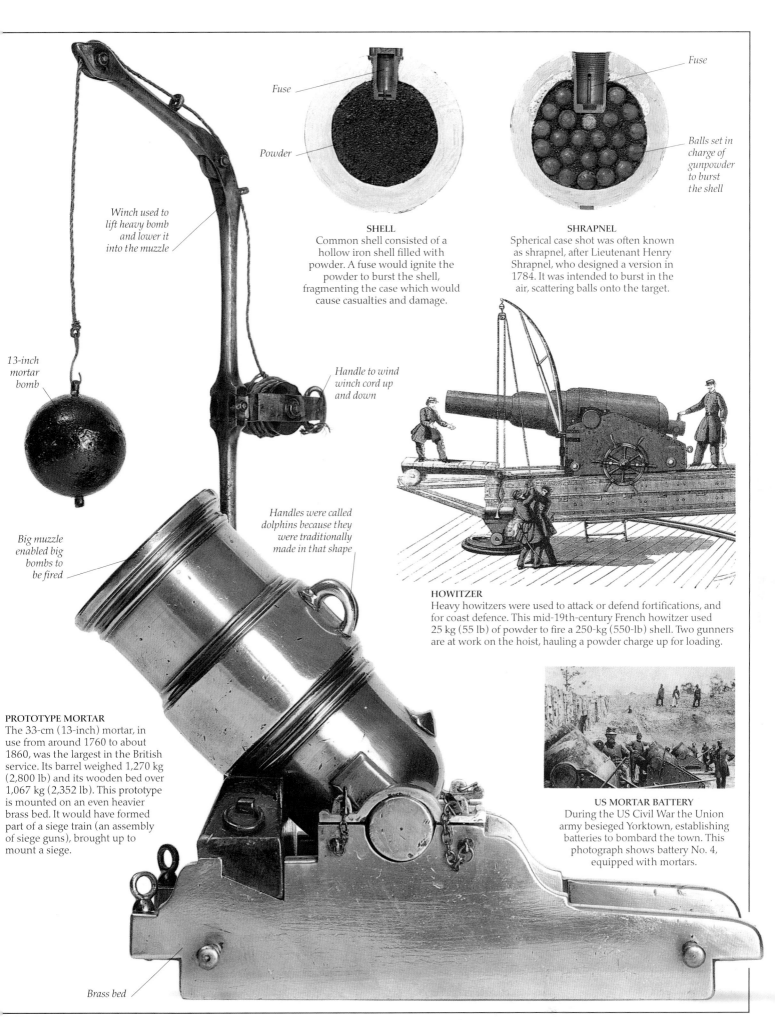

Fuse

Powder

SHELL
Common shell consisted of a hollow iron shell filled with powder. A fuse would ignite the powder to burst the shell, fragmenting the case which would cause casualties and damage.

Fuse

Balls set in charge of gunpowder to burst the shell

SHRAPNEL
Spherical case shot was often known as shrapnel, after Lieutenant Henry Shrapnel, who designed a version in 1784. It was intended to burst in the air, scattering balls onto the target.

Winch used to lift heavy bomb and lower it into the muzzle

13-inch mortar bomb

Handle to wind winch cord up and down

Big muzzle enabled big bombs to be fired

Handles were called dolphins because they were traditionally made in that shape

HOWITZER
Heavy howitzers were used to attack or defend fortifications, and for coast defence. This mid-19th-century French howitzer used 25 kg (55 lb) of powder to fire a 250-kg (550-lb) shell. Two gunners are at work on the hoist, hauling a powder charge up for loading.

PROTOTYPE MORTAR
The 33-cm (13-inch) mortar, in use from around 1760 to about 1860, was the largest in the British service. Its barrel weighed 1,270 kg (2,800 lb) and its wooden bed over 1,067 kg (2,352 lb). This prototype is mounted on an even heavier brass bed. It would have formed part of a siege train (an assembly of siege guns), brought up to mount a siege.

US MORTAR BATTERY
During the US Civil War the Union army besieged Yorktown, establishing batteries to bombard the town. This photograph shows battery No. 4, equipped with mortars.

Brass bed

Artillery instruments

EARLY CANNON WERE CUMBERSOME and inaccurate. Prussian gunners maintained that "the first shot is for God, the second is for the devil, and only the third is for the king." In the earliest textbook on gunnery (1537) Niccolo Tartaglia described the relationship between the speed of the cannonball and the path it followed, writing "the more swift the pellet doth fly, the less crooked is its range". To make the most of their cannon, gunners needed instruments to position them correctly. They used quadrants to find the angle of elevation and calculate how far a shot would go. Rules enabled them to measure a cannon's muzzle to establish the weight of ball it fired, levels helped them to place guns precisely upright, and they used dividers to measure ranges on maps.

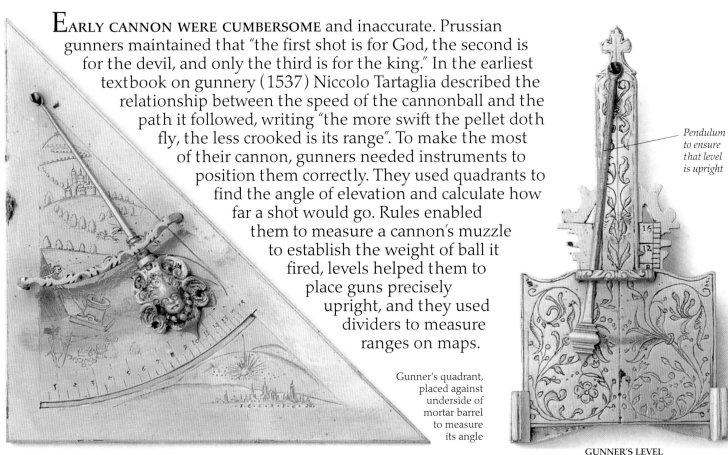

Pendulum to ensure that level is upright

Gunner's quadrant, placed against underside of mortar barrel to measure its angle

GUNNER'S LEVEL
This level was shaped to stand on the breech of a cannon: when the pendulum was central, the gun was standing level.

VENT CLEANERS
Instruments of this sort often fitted in the scabbard of the elaborate sword sometimes carried by master gunners.

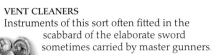

Studs protect the pole from wear, as well as holding the quadrant in place

Label shows which sort of shot the scale is for, in this case, gravel

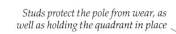

SLAG

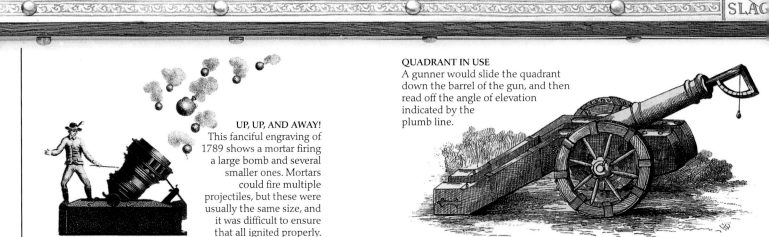

UP, UP, AND AWAY!
This fanciful engraving of 1789 shows a mortar firing a large bomb and several smaller ones. Mortars could fire multiple projectiles, but these were usually the same size, and it was difficult to ensure that all ignited properly.

QUADRANT IN USE
A gunner would slide the quadrant down the barrel of the gun, and then read off the angle of elevation indicated by the plumb line.

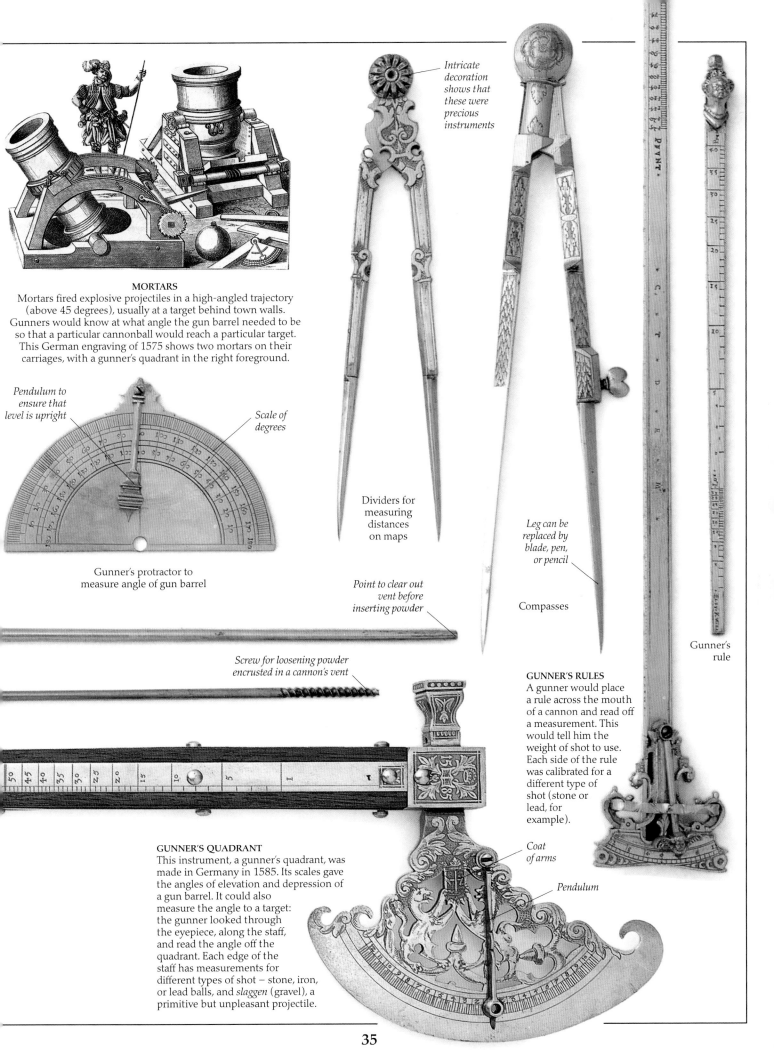

Intricate decoration shows that these were precious instruments

MORTARS

Mortars fired explosive projectiles in a high-angled trajectory (above 45 degrees), usually at a target behind town walls. Gunners would know at what angle the gun barrel needed to be so that a particular cannonball would reach a particular target. This German engraving of 1575 shows two mortars on their carriages, with a gunner's quadrant in the right foreground.

Pendulum to ensure that level is upright

Scale of degrees

Gunner's protractor to measure angle of gun barrel

Dividers for measuring distances on maps

Leg can be replaced by blade, pen, or pencil

Compasses

Point to clear out vent before inserting powder

Screw for loosening powder encrusted in a cannon's vent

Gunner's rule

GUNNER'S RULES

A gunner would place a rule across the mouth of a cannon and read off a measurement. This would tell him the weight of shot to use. Each side of the rule was calibrated for a different type of shot (stone or lead, for example).

Coat of arms

Pendulum

GUNNER'S QUADRANT

This instrument, a gunner's quadrant, was made in Germany in 1585. Its scales gave the angles of elevation and depression of a gun barrel. It could also measure the angle to a target: the gunner looked through the eyepiece, along the staff, and read the angle off the quadrant. Each edge of the staff has measurements for different types of shot – stone, iron, or lead balls, and *slaggen* (gravel), a primitive but unpleasant projectile.

Bows and arrows

WEAPONS THAT WERE SHOT and thrown enabled their users to attack an opponent from a distance. Bows played a major role in battle. The longbow, made of wood or a combination of materials like wood and horn, was deadly in skilled hands and could even send its arrow through some types of armour. However, it took years of practice to use one effectively. The crossbow was more powerful than the longbow, but was heavier and had a slower rate of fire. Both longbow and crossbow were used in medieval Europe. Thrown weapons including javelins (throwing spears) were used by people all over the world, such as Romans, African peoples, and Aboriginal Australians. Hand-grenades came into use in the 17th century, and did more damage than other thrown weapons by exploding on impact.

FIREWORKS
Arrows tipped with inflammable compounds could be shot into wooden buildings or on to thatched roofs to cause fires. These 17th-century illustrations (above and right) show slightly fanciful versions of flaming arrows.

Armour-piercing bodkin point

Gap in arrowhead made it lighter

Barb

Painted, gilt, and lacquered decoration

Strong, flexible bamboo shaft

Thickened tip for piercing light armour

INDIAN ARROWS
An archer would use an appropriate arrowhead for his target. Armour-piercing "bodkin points" were sharp and narrow, while other heads were broader. Arrows often had barbs to make them harder to extract. The elaborate decoration on these arrows show that they belonged to someone of high rank.

LONGBOWMEN
In the 14th and 15th centuries, archers, trained from youth to use the longbow, were the prime instrument of English victory over the French in battles in the Hundred Years War (1337–1453) like Crécy, Poitiers, and Agincourt. This was mainly because French knights, used to hand-to-hand combat, were killed by the longbowmen as they charged towards successive hails of arrows.

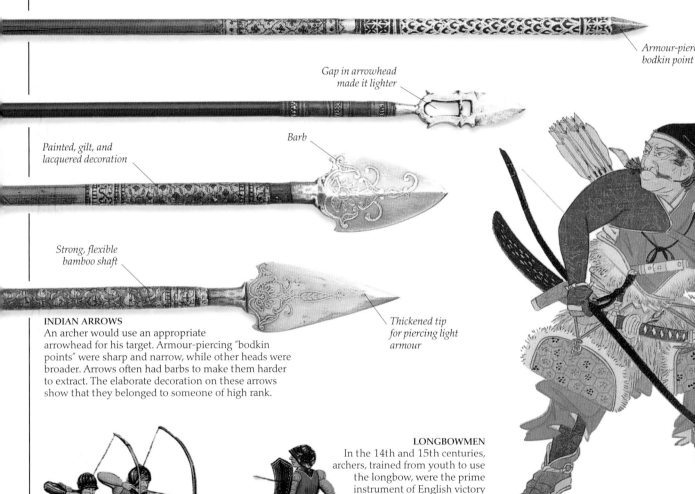

JAPANESE ARCHER
Japanese war bows were made of bamboo and other wood combined, and were longer than European longbows. Whereas a European knight would have considered it beneath his dignity to use a bow in battle, many samurai were skilled archers. They were trained from childhood to follow a strict code called the "warrior's way", and were prepared to fight to death for their overlord.

CROSSBOW

The crossbow was popular in medieval Europe, and versions were used in China and Japan. In some lighter models the string was drawn back by means of a hook called a goat's-foot lever. Usually the bow was so powerful that its user needed a small winch, called a moulinet, to draw it. When the bow was drawn the moulinet was removed and the bolt was loaded. The crossbow was powerful and accurate, but it was slow to load and hard to protect from rain or damp. At Crécy (1346) the Genoese crossbowmen on the French side were outshot by English longbowmen.

BOOMERANG

The boomerang is a curved throwing-stick used for fighting or hunting by the Aboriginal Australians. Although some boomerangs were specially designed to return to the thrower, many were not. Similar weapons were used in Africa and India.

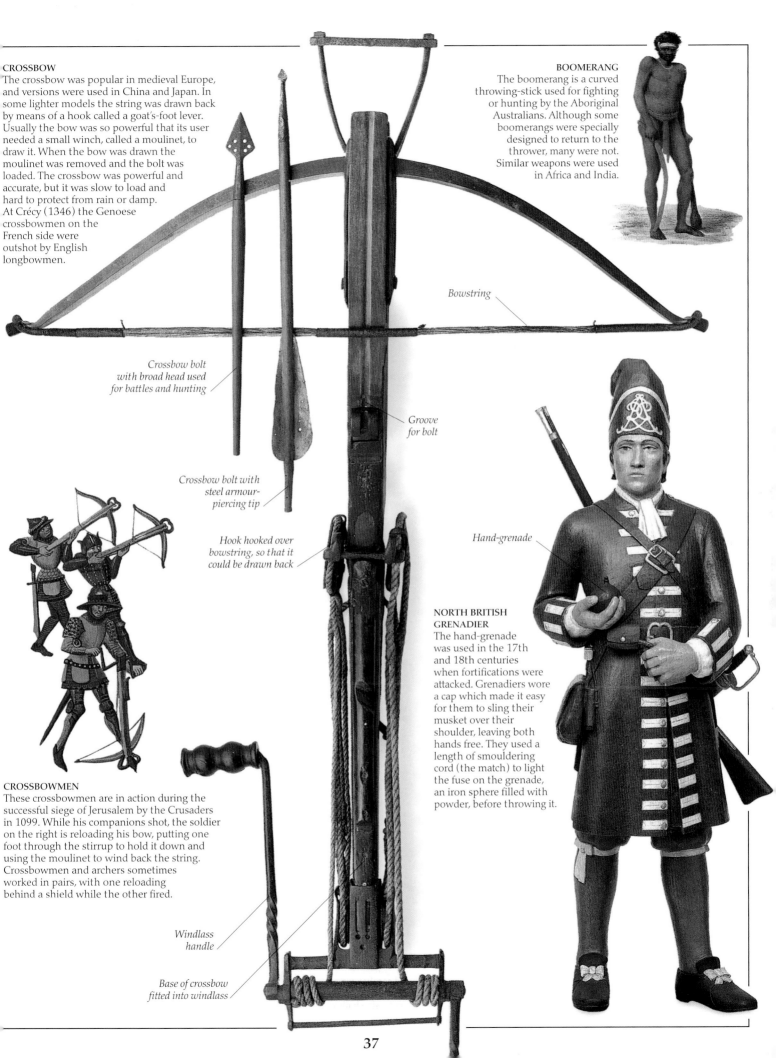

Bowstring

Crossbow bolt with broad head used for battles and hunting

Groove for bolt

Crossbow bolt with steel armour-piercing tip

Hook hooked over bowstring, so that it could be drawn back

Hand-grenade

NORTH BRITISH GRENADIER

The hand-grenade was used in the 17th and 18th centuries when fortifications were attacked. Grenadiers wore a cap which made it easy for them to sling their musket over their shoulder, leaving both hands free. They used a length of smouldering cord (the match) to light the fuse on the grenade, an iron sphere filled with powder, before throwing it.

CROSSBOWMEN

These crossbowmen are in action during the successful siege of Jerusalem by the Crusaders in 1099. While his companions shot, the soldier on the right is reloading his bow, putting one foot through the stirrup to hold it down and using the moulinet to wind back the string. Crossbowmen and archers sometimes worked in pairs, with one reloading behind a shield while the other fired.

Windlass handle

Base of crossbow fitted into windlass

Maces and battle-axes

WIDELY USED BY KNIGHTS and warriors from the 11th to the 16th centuries, maces and battle-axes could be used to smash their way through helmets and body armour as well as chain mail. While armour offered good protection against edged weapons like swords or spears, some daggers were specially designed to defeat armour by penetrating where plates joined. It could be difficult to kill a dismounted knight if the right weapon was not to hand: at the battle of Bouvines, fought in 1214 near Lille in northern France, the French King Philip Augustus was surrounded by enemy footsoldiers, but they failed to kill him before help arrived.

Armour-piercing spike

Flange

Long handle gave the user extra "swing"

Weighted head helped the user to strike harder

Hammer head

Spike for penetrating armour

WAR HAMMER
The war hammer was a popular weapon in Europe. It usually had a sharp point at the back, and a blunt head or a set of claws which would not slip on armour, at the front. This specimen is Polish or Hungarian and dates from about 1700.

SPIKED MACE
Helmets were often designed to encourage blows to glance off them. This 18th-century Indian mace is embellished with spikes which would prevent it from slipping when it struck. Cruder spiked weapons – called "morning stars" or "holy water sprinklers" – were used in Europe.

Ornamental studs

Grip

Top of handle protects hand

FLANGED MACE
This mace, made in Italy in about 1550, has the weight to smash armour, and flanges which help it to penetrate the armour. Maces were often hung from a knight's saddle when not in use. They were sometimes carried by fighting clerics (churchmen) who were forbidden to shed blood!

WARRIOR MONK
Most Japanese warriors carried a two-handed Japanese sword that had a sharp, heavy blade. However, this redoubtable warrior monk is armed with a mighty club. These monks wore a mixture of military and monkish dress, with a cap instead of a helmet.

PUNCHING DAGGER

The Indian fist-dagger was held by the grip which runs at right angles to the blade, so that the blow was delivered by punching. This late-18th-century version has a double blade, but single blades with reinforced points for the penetration of armour were more common.

Wrist-guard

Grip

Serrated blades caused more damage to armour and opponent

Armour-piercing points

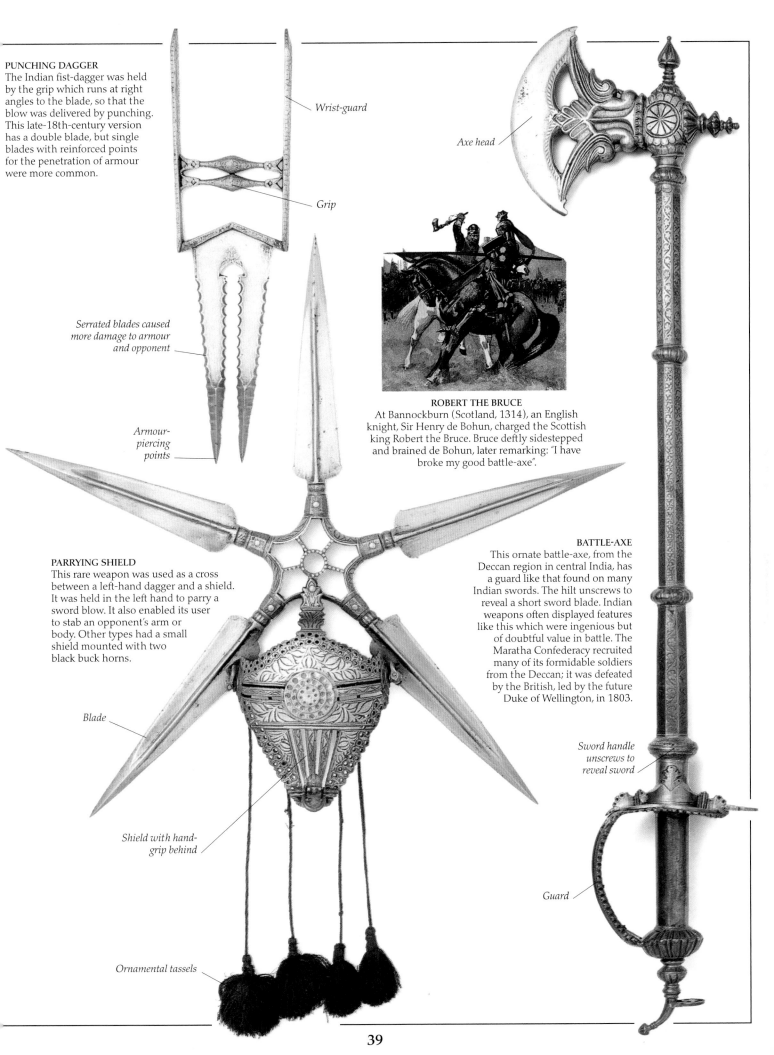

ROBERT THE BRUCE
At Bannockburn (Scotland, 1314), an English knight, Sir Henry de Bohun, charged the Scottish king Robert the Bruce. Bruce deftly sidestepped and brained de Bohun, later remarking: "I have broke my good battle-axe".

Axe head

PARRYING SHIELD

This rare weapon was used as a cross between a left-hand dagger and a shield. It was held in the left hand to parry a sword blow. It also enabled its user to stab an opponent's arm or body. Other types had a small shield mounted with two black buck horns.

Blade

Shield with hand-grip behind

Ornamental tassels

BATTLE-AXE

This ornate battle-axe, from the Deccan region in central India, has a guard like that found on many Indian swords. The hilt unscrews to reveal a short sword blade. Indian weapons often displayed features like this which were ingenious but of doubtful value in battle. The Maratha Confederacy recruited many of its formidable soldiers from the Deccan; it was defeated by the British, led by the future Duke of Wellington, in 1803.

Sword handle unscrews to reveal sword

Guard

39

Swords

THE SWORD WAS USED in prehistoric times, and was still carried by cavalrymen as late as the end of World War I (1914–1918). There were two main types of sword. Cutting swords, such as medieval knights' cross-hilted swords or Highland officers' broadswords, had heavy blades with sharp edges. Stabbing swords, like the rapier, were lighter and had sharp points. Many military swords were general purpose "cut and thrust" weapons. Real damage in battle was usually done by well-directed thrusts which produced lethal wounds, rather than by cuts which were often deflected by an opponent's helmet.

Hand and wrist fit inside steel gauntlet, which is held by a grip inside

SWORD DRILL
To use his sword effectively a soldier had to know how to attack his enemy, and to protect himself by parries (defensive strokes). This series of illustrations comes from an early-19th-century British drill-book and shows exercises for the broadsword.

LADIES FIGHTING
This 15th-century lady is wielding a knightly broadsword. Although women rarely took up arms in medieval Europe, in Japan women of samurai families were sometimes trained to use a light halberd (p. 45).

SWORD-BREAKER
When men fought on foot with rapiers, they often carried a dagger in the left hand. A sword-breaker was also carried in the left hand, and its serrated edge was intended to catch an opponent's blade, which could then be broken with a twist of the wrist. It could also be used as a conventional dagger. This example was made in Italy in about 1660.

GAUNTLET SWORD
A fighter's sword hand and forearm were in danger from an opponent's cuts. This 17th-century Indian gauntlet sword embodied protection for the hand and the wrist. Its blade was made in Solingen, a centre of sword-production in Germany. Good-quality European blades were often used in Asia, and vice versa: attractively patterned "Damascus" blades are sometimes found on 19th-century European swords.

Solingen maker's mark

Barbs to trap opponent's blade

Sharp edge

Broad, double-edged blade

CAVALRY CHARGE

Heavy cavalry usually carried straight, heavy swords and were trained to use them primarily for thrusting, leaning forward in the saddle with the sword-arm outstretched. This illustration shows a famous German cavalry charge, known as "Von Bredow's Death-Ride", that took place in 1870 in the Franco-Prussian War. In practice, at that time, the infantry soldier who kept his head and used his rifle and bayonet to defend himself had a good chance of beating a cavalryman.

Guard

Grip

Pommel

PAPPENHEIMER RAPIER

This rapier was named after the Graf zu Pappenheim, a general in the Thirty Years War (1618–1648) between the Catholic and Protestant forces in most of Europe. The complex hilt, with a combination of shell-shaped guards covering the hand and bars protecting the knuckles, was characteristic of this type of sword.

BROADSWORD

This basket-hilted broadsword was carried by Scottish Highland officers at the time when infantry still used swords in battle. It is sometimes called a claymore, although that name initially referred to an earlier broadsword with a cross-shaped guard.

A groove called a fuller added strength to blade; it was also less correctly known as a blood gutter

Maker's mark

Buckskin covered with red cloth

Pierced steel guard offers good protection

Firearms

IN THE 18TH AND 19TH centuries, most infantry soldiers carried a musket. This had a smooth-bore barrel and was loaded by inserting powder and shot into the muzzle and ramming it home. It had a short range and its black powder produced acrid smoke. A few specialists were equipped with rifles, whose barrels, cut with spiral grooves, spun the bullet to improve its range and accuracy. Inventors had long experimented with breech-loading (rear-loading) weapons, but it was not until the middle of the 19th century that these became available on a large scale. Bayonets could be fitted to the weapon's muzzle for close-quarter fighting.

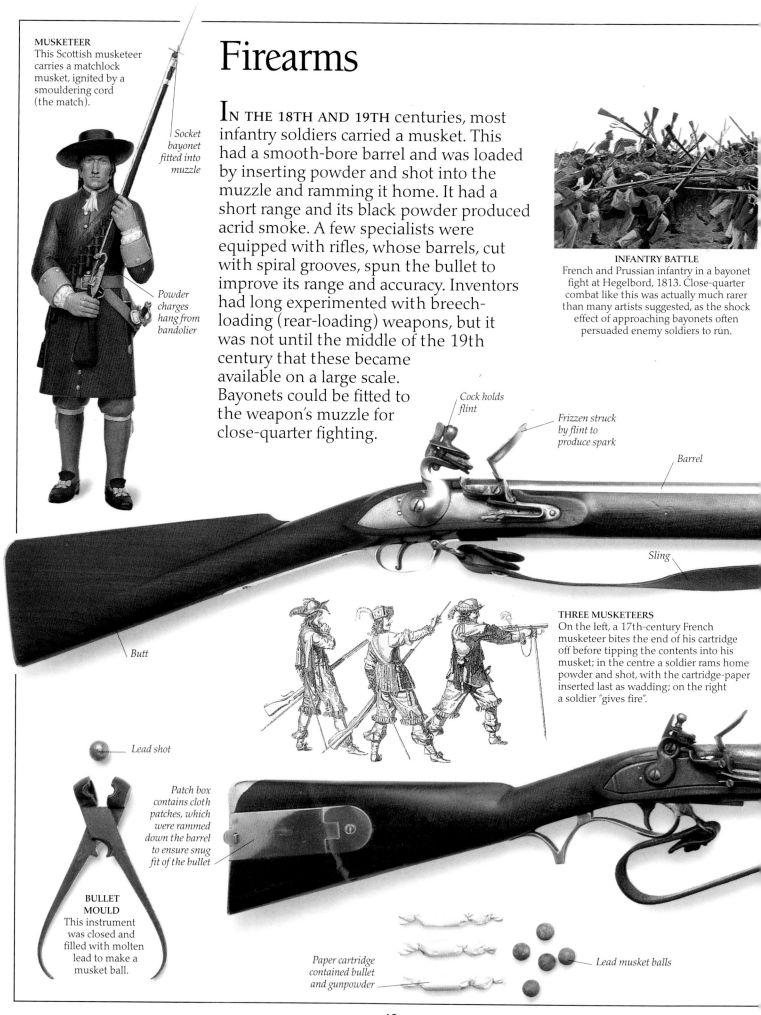

MUSKETEER
This Scottish musketeer carries a matchlock musket, ignited by a smouldering cord (the match).

Socket bayonet fitted into muzzle

Powder charges hang from bandolier

INFANTRY BATTLE
French and Prussian infantry in a bayonet fight at Hegelbord, 1813. Close-quarter combat like this was actually much rarer than many artists suggested, as the shock effect of approaching bayonets often persuaded enemy soldiers to run.

Cock holds flint

Frizzen struck by flint to produce spark

Barrel

Sling

Butt

THREE MUSKETEERS
On the left, a 17th-century French musketeer bites the end of his cartridge off before tipping the contents into his musket; in the centre a soldier rams home powder and shot, with the cartridge-paper inserted last as wadding; on the right a soldier "gives fire".

Lead shot

Patch box contains cloth patches, which were rammed down the barrel to ensure snug fit of the bullet

BULLET MOULD
This instrument was closed and filled with molten lead to make a musket ball.

Paper cartridge contained bullet and gunpowder

Lead musket balls

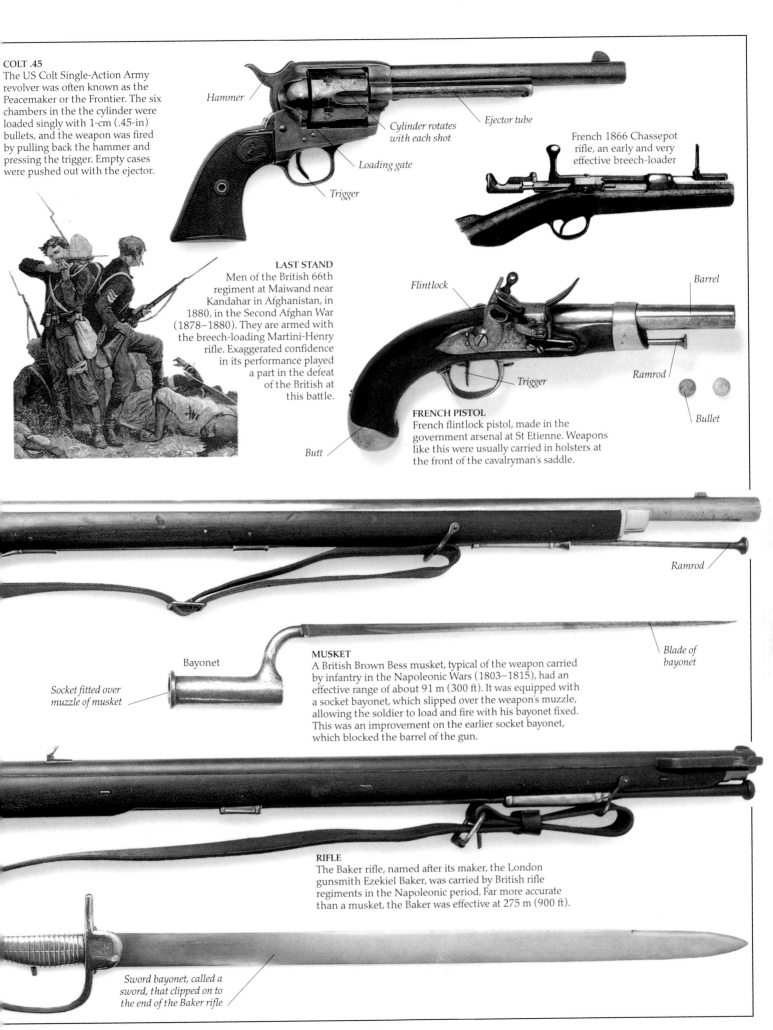

COLT .45
The US Colt Single-Action Army revolver was often known as the Peacemaker or the Frontier. The six chambers in the the cylinder were loaded singly with 1-cm (.45-in) bullets, and the weapon was fired by pulling back the hammer and pressing the trigger. Empty cases were pushed out with the ejector.

Hammer

Cylinder rotates with each shot

Ejector tube

Loading gate

Trigger

French 1866 Chassepot rifle, an early and very effective breech-loader

LAST STAND
Men of the British 66th regiment at Maiwand near Kandahar in Afghanistan, in 1880, in the Second Afghan War (1878–1880). They are armed with the breech-loading Martini-Henry rifle. Exaggerated confidence in its performance played a part in the defeat of the British at this battle.

Flintlock

Barrel

Trigger

Ramrod

Bullet

Butt

FRENCH PISTOL
French flintlock pistol, made in the government arsenal at St Etienne. Weapons like this were usually carried in holsters at the front of the cavalryman's saddle.

Ramrod

Blade of bayonet

Bayonet

Socket fitted over muzzle of musket

MUSKET
A British Brown Bess musket, typical of the weapon carried by infantry in the Napoleonic Wars (1803–1815), had an effective range of about 91 m (300 ft). It was equipped with a socket bayonet, which slipped over the weapon's muzzle, allowing the soldier to load and fire with his bayonet fixed. This was an improvement on the earlier socket bayonet, which blocked the barrel of the gun.

RIFLE
The Baker rifle, named after its maker, the London gunsmith Ezekiel Baker, was carried by British rifle regiments in the Napoleonic period. Far more accurate than a musket, the Baker was effective at 275 m (900 ft).

Sword bayonet, called a sword, that clipped on to the end of the Baker rifle

Close combat

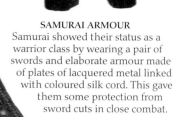

STORM FROM THE EAST
Successive waves of invaders from Asia threatened Europe. These Mongol horsemen (p. 14), entirely at home in the saddle, were formidable opponents.

Ancient battles were contests between warriors on foot or horseback. They struck out in close combat with bronze or iron weapons, and used short-range missiles like arrows or javelins. Although battle tactics were usually simple, some commanders showed special skill, for example, by keeping a reserve of fresh troops at hand and using them when the enemy was exhausted. More often training or equipment gave the decisive advantage: the Roman army and the Greeks of Alexander the Great (356–323 BCE) were well armed and well organized, and used carefully thought-out tactics. For thousands of years the infantry were superior, but with the invention of the stirrup the cavalry reigned almost unchecked until the development of firearms.

Repair indicates that it was worn through many battles

Crest helped to deflect blows from enemy's sword

SAMURAI ARMOUR
Samurai showed their status as a warrior class by wearing a pair of swords and elaborate armour made of plates of lacquered metal linked with coloured silk cord. This gave them some protection from sword cuts in close combat.

WARRIOR QUEEN
Not all women stayed at home while their menfolk were hunters and warriors. In the first century CE, Boudicca, the queen of a tribe living in East Anglia (England), fought against the occupying Romans. Although she destroyed three of the Romans' most important towns (London, St Albans, and Colchester), she was eventually defeated by the Romans' superior tactics.

PRE-ETRUSCAN HELMET
Armour protected a soldier's most vulnerable points, and therefore added greatly to his chances of survival, but at the same time the weight slowed him down. This bronze helmet comes from Vulci in Italy and was made between 800 and 700 BCE. Although at this time iron had been introduced in Europe, bronze was still used for armour and weapons alike.

"Recover your halberd"

"Advance your halberd"

"Shoulder your halberd"

HALBERD DRILL
Weapons with a blade or a spike on a long wooden handle are called pole arms or staff weapons. A weapon of this type, the halberd, survived from medieval times to become the characteristic weapon of European infantry sergeants throughout the 18th century. These figures demonstrate halberd drill.

POLISH MACE
In the 17th century, Poland fielded impressive heavy cavalry who used lances, as well as maces like this early 17th-century specimen. The Polish king John Sobieski (1624–1696) led the army which beat the Turks besieging Vienna in 1683, a victory which helped keep most of Europe out of Turkish control.

Swiss halberd, from around 1400

German pole-axe, early 16th century

Maker's mark

Sharp edge

REACHING OUT
Pole-axes and halberds increased the infantry soldiers' reach and were very useful if they were dealing with horsemen. The Swiss gained an awesome reputation by using pikemen who carried long spears, assisted by halberdiers. Charles the Bold, Duke of Burgundy (1433–1477), was killed in battle against the Swiss at Nancy, his head split open by a halberd blow.

Langets (metal strips) protect staff

Mounted knights carry steel-tipped lances and a pennant

KNIGHT IN ARMOUR
Armoured knights, charging with lances on their heavy horses, were the dominant force in medieval Europe. There were some foes, like Swiss pikemen or English archers, whom they found hard to deal with. Monarchs liked to be depicted as knights even when these warriors were losing their value: this illustration shows the Emperor Charles V of Spain in 1529.

Gunpowder arms

THE INVENTION OF GUNPOWDER, a mixture of explosive chemicals, led to the invention of firearms. In these weapons a controlled explosion of gunpowder in one part of the firearm sent a bullet or a cannonball down a barrel. In fact gunpowder did not change war at a stroke: in the 16th and 17th centuries a mixture of old and new techniques were used in battles, with swords and pikes alongside muskets and cannon. For most of that period infantry and cavalry alike used firearms and edged weapons. Infantry consisted of pikemen, with body armour and long spears, and musketeers armed with muskets. Cavalrymen carried swords and pistols, but the steady increase of infantry firepower limited their effectiveness. Most armies drew up with their infantry in the centre and the cavalry on the flanks. Cannon, still relatively cumbersome and primitive, were placed in the gaps between blocks of infantry.

FIRING A VOLLEY
Volley guns or "ribaldequins" had numerous barrels that were fired more or less simultaneously. In this specimen, shown in a French publication of 1630, the gunner fires the barrels one at a time.

OLIVER CROMWELL
Cromwell (1599–1658) was an English country gentleman and Member of Parliament who helped raise the Parliamentarian army on the outbreak of the Civil War in 1642. He became lieutenant-general (second-in-command) of the New Model Army and played a leading role in winning the decisive battle of Naseby (1645).

Cock (with flint) lowered onto revolving wheel

PISTOLS
Musket, with their longer barrels, were difficult to use on horseback. The first pistols, which were hand-held weapons, were wheel-lock pistols. The wheel was wound up with a key, and when the trigger was pressed it revolved, striking sparks from a flint held in the cock.

Revolving wheel with toothed edge

Trigger

Ring for carrying cord

Rammer, to force charge and bullet down gunbarrel

Nozzle

Spanner to wind up wheel on pistol

POWDER FLASK
The nozzle of this powder flask has two spring-loaded catches. The one nearer the flask was opened to let powder flow into the nozzle. It was then closed, trapping a measured quantity of powder, which was loaded into the weapon by opening the upper catch.

GUSTAVUS ADOLPHUS
The Thirty Years War (1618–1648), in which Protestants fought Catholics, was the most destructive conflict of the period in Europe. The Swedish king Gustavus Adolphus (1594–1632) was a champion of the Protestant cause. He produced a reliable professional army which he commanded with skill and courage, only to be killed at Lützen, half-way through the conflict.

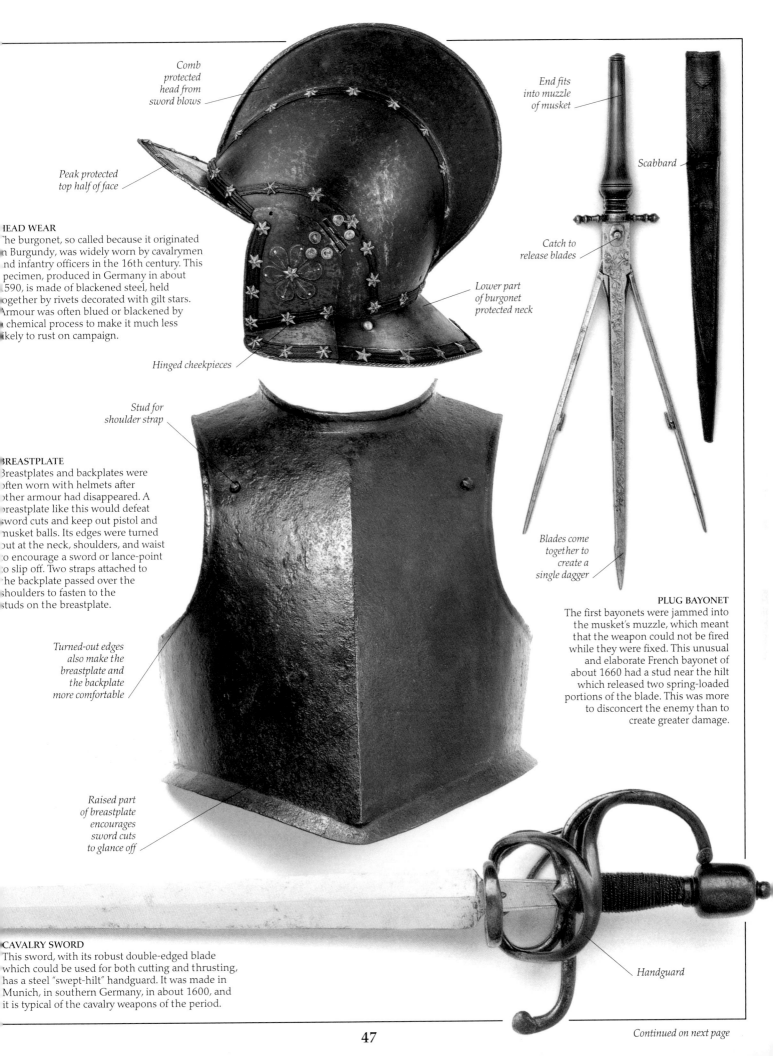

Comb protected head from sword blows

End fits into muzzle of musket

Scabbard

Peak protected top half of face

HEAD WEAR
The burgonet, so called because it originated in Burgundy, was widely worn by cavalrymen and infantry officers in the 16th century. This specimen, produced in Germany in about 1590, is made of blackened steel, held together by rivets decorated with gilt stars. Armour was often blued or blackened by a chemical process to make it much less likely to rust on campaign.

Catch to release blades

Lower part of burgonet protected neck

Hinged cheekpieces

Stud for shoulder strap

BREASTPLATE
Breastplates and backplates were often worn with helmets after other armour had disappeared. A breastplate like this would defeat sword cuts and keep out pistol and musket balls. Its edges were turned out at the neck, shoulders, and waist to encourage a sword or lance-point to slip off. Two straps attached to the backplate passed over the shoulders to fasten to the studs on the breastplate.

Blades come together to create a single dagger

PLUG BAYONET
The first bayonets were jammed into the musket's muzzle, which meant that the weapon could not be fired while they were fixed. This unusual and elaborate French bayonet of about 1660 had a stud near the hilt which released two spring-loaded portions of the blade. This was more to disconcert the enemy than to create greater damage.

Turned-out edges also make the breastplate and the backplate more comfortable

Raised part of breastplate encourages sword cuts to glance off

CAVALRY SWORD
This sword, with its robust double-edged blade which could be used for both cutting and thrusting, has a steel "swept-hilt" handguard. It was made in Munich, in southern Germany, in about 1600, and it is typical of the cavalry weapons of the period.

Handguard

Continued on next page

Large armies

In the early 18th century, battles took on a form they were to retain for many years. The majority of combatants were foot soldiers (infantry) armed with flintlock muskets, and battles centred on ferocious close-range exchanges of fire between the opposing infantrymen. Light cavalry scouted, screened (carried out counter-reconnaissance activities), and pursued, and heavy cavalry charged hostile horsemen and rode down shaken infantry. Cannonballs, multiple shot, and shells caused dreadful casualties in the enemy's close-packed ranks. For most of the 18th century, armies were composed of both volunteers and men pressed into service. Frederick the Great (1712–1786) tried to recruit foreigners so as not to ruin Prussian industry and agriculture: in 1768 he had 70,000 native soldiers in an army of 160,000. The French Revolution changed all this. In 1793 the Revolutionary government, threatened by invasion, declared that all able-bodied men were to serve, and the army may have reached a million men in mid-1794, ushering in the age of mass armies.

Cartridge top held safely in place by button

AMMUNITION POUCH
This white metal pouch was made in the Caucasus in the late 18th century and would have contained paper cartridges for a musket or a pistol. There is a clip at the back for attaching it to the belt.

CARTRIDGE CASE
This cartridge case is one of a pair that buttoned onto its owner's coat. In the heat of action, it was important to have easy access to ammunition. Russian Cossacks wore these as late as World War II.

PISTOLS
Many cavalrymen carried a pair of pistols in holsters at the front of their saddles. These were made in the Caucasus, an area subject to Russian and Turkish influence, and are decorated with embossed silverwork that has a rather Asian appearance.

LIGHT DRAGOON
This private of the British 13th Light Dragoons is practising parrying, or defelecting, a cut aimed at his horse's head by an enemy horseman. His curved sabre is typical of that carried by light cavalry, who used their swords for cutting rather than thrusting. His carbine (a short musket) would normally have been clipped to the carbine belt passing over his left shoulder. The 13th served with the Duke of Wellington in Spain in the Peninsular War (1808–1814).

NAPOLEON
Napoleon Bonaparte (1769–1821) was an artillery officer who became Emperor of the French in 1804. He dominated Europe, winning a series of victories, but exhausted his army when they retreated from Moscow in Russia's inhospitable winter (1812), and was then defeated at Waterloo (1815). He was brilliantly successful in using corps (large groups of regiments of all arms) which moved on separate routes but fought united.

DETTINGEN
In 1743 an Allied army under George II beat the French at Dettingen on the River Main. It was the last time a king of England commanded in battle. Contemporary illustrations fail to show just how smoky battlefields were. A veteran of an earlier battle saw no light "but what the fire of the volleys of shot gave".

2.7-kg (6-lb) cannonball

CANNONBALLS
Solid shot was the most common artillery projectile. Gunners usually tried to obtain a ricochet effect: they fired cannonballs which hit the ground just in front of their target and then bounced through it, causing casualties with every bound. This technique required firm ground, and the effect of Napoleon's main battery of guns at Waterloo was spoilt by soggy terrain.

Bronze gun barrel

BURMESE DRAGON
Superior military technology sometimes gave European armies a decisive advantage when they were fighting overseas, although determined local people who knew the ground proved serious adversaries. Asian and African rulers sometimes hired European military experts and bought modern weapons. This cannon was made in Portugal for the King of Burma (now Myanmar). It is a decorative piece but would have worked had the need arisen. The barrel was captured by the British in 1885 and is mounted on a replacement carriage.

Replacement gun carriage

Rifled weapons

FROM THE MID-19TH CENTURY onwards, technology changed the face of battle. Weapons gained accuracy by becoming rifled (with a grooved barrel), and rate of fire by becoming breech-loading (back-loading). Black powder was replaced by smokeless powder, and new high explosives increased the effect of shells. Machine guns developed into mobile weapons which provided "the concentrated essence of infantry". It took armies some time to assimilate the effects of new technology, but the firepower revolution eventually produced battlefields which seemed strangely empty: by World War I (1914–1918) whole armies took refuge in trenches. A British artillery officer wrote that "there were thousands of hidden men in front of me ... but nobody moved, everybody was waiting for the safety of darkness".

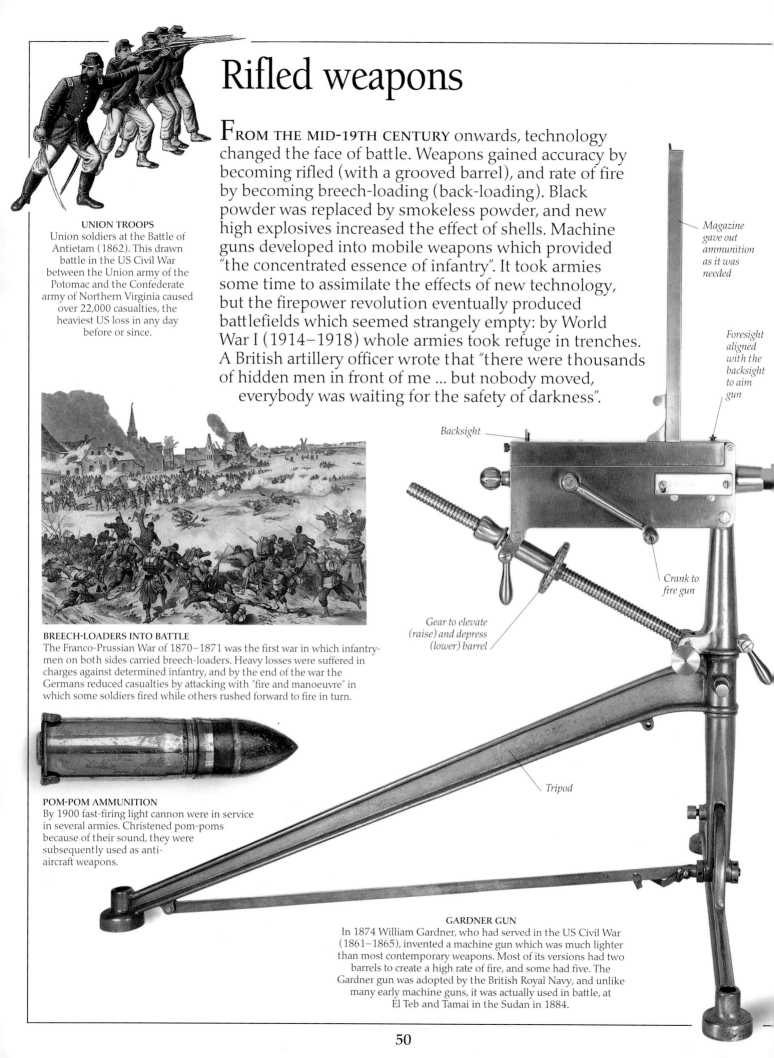

UNION TROOPS
Union soldiers at the Battle of Antietam (1862). This drawn battle in the US Civil War between the Union army of the Potomac and the Confederate army of Northern Virginia caused over 22,000 casualties, the heaviest US loss in any day before or since.

Magazine gave out ammunition as it was needed

Foresight aligned with the backsight to aim gun

Backsight

Crank to fire gun

Gear to elevate (raise) and depress (lower) barrel

Tripod

BREECH-LOADERS INTO BATTLE
The Franco-Prussian War of 1870–1871 was the first war in which infantry-men on both sides carried breech-loaders. Heavy losses were suffered in charges against determined infantry, and by the end of the war the Germans reduced casualties by attacking with "fire and manoeuvre" in which some soldiers fired while others rushed forward to fire in turn.

POM-POM AMMUNITION
By 1900 fast-firing light cannon were in service in several armies. Christened pom-poms because of their sound, they were subsequently used as anti-aircraft weapons.

GARDNER GUN
In 1874 William Gardner, who had served in the US Civil War (1861–1865), invented a machine gun which was much lighter than most contemporary weapons. Most of its versions had two barrels to create a high rate of fire, and some had five. The Gardner gun was adopted by the British Royal Navy, and unlike many early machine guns, it was actually used in battle, at El Teb and Tamai in the Sudan in 1884.

LEE-ENFIELD RIFLE

In 1902 the British army adopted the .303-in Lee-Enfield short magazine rifle as the best and latest technology. A trained soldier could fire at least 15 rounds a minute with it, and it had an effective range of up to 1,097 m (3,600 ft).

Sword bayonet

BOER BANDOLIER

Ammunition consisting of smokeless powder in metallic cases was easy to carry and store.

INDIAN WARS

In the 1870s, US cavalrymen used single-shot Springfield carbines, but discovered that some of their opponents had traded hides for much-superior Winchester repeaters.

US cavalrymen in action during the Indian Wars of the 1870s

RIFLED BARREL

Rifling describes the grooves in a weapon's barrel which spin the bullet to make it go further faster. There were many systems. This is the Whitworth hexagonal system, used in some British-made cannon imported by the Confederates during the US Civil War.

Twisted grooves

BATTLE OF FORT WAGNER

Slavery helped cause the US Civil War, as slavery was banned in the North but important for working on plantations in the South. The Union army (of the North) used black soldiers in segregated regiments with white officers. 5,000 Union soldiers, including the 54th Massachusetts (Colored) Volunteers, attacked Fort Wagner on Charleston harbour on 18 July 1863. They reached the fort but could not take it, and lost 1,500 men.

ROBERT E. LEE

Lee (1807–1870) commanded the main Confederate army (of the South) during the US Civil War. He defended Northern Virginia, preventing superior Union armies from taking the Confederate capital of Richmond, and invaded the North twice.

Communications

HELIOGRAPH
The heliograph, a tripod-mounted mirror, used sunlight to create flashes. Long and short flashes made up letters of the alphabet. It worked well in areas like the northwest frontier of India which were often sunny and had long views.

Sight

A heliograph's mirror could be adjusted to send messages in any direction

Tripod

THE US GENERAL Omar Bradley (1893–1981) wrote that "Congress makes a man a general: communications make him a commander". On the battlefield itself, soldiers needed to communicate, although their ability to do so was impeded by noise, smoke, and confusion. Senior commanders had to know what was happening in battle in order to commit fresh troops or change their line of attack. Often inadequate communications, not lack of skill or courage, ruined a promising plan. Until the development of the telegraph in the mid-19th century, communications changed little. Staff officers or messengers delivered verbal or written messages. Regimental officers used their own voices or relayed orders through drummers and trumpeters. Messages could be sent over longer distances by signalling systems or heliographs.

PIGEONS FOR RECONNAISSANCE
French cavalry in 1897 sending messages by carrier pigeons. Their main limitation was that they simply flew back to their lofts, so messages could only be sent one way.

MESSAGE CARRIERS
Pigeons with messages attached to their legs in carriers like these were widely used during World War I, when the largely static nature of trench warfare reduced their limitations. The last message sent from Fort Vaux at Verdun, fiercely attacked by the Germans in 1916, asked for help and warned: "This is my last pigeon."

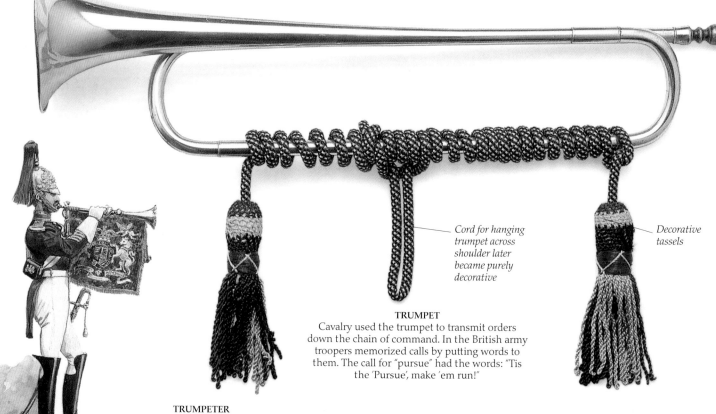

Cord for hanging trumpet across shoulder later became purely decorative

Decorative tassels

TRUMPET
Cavalry used the trumpet to transmit orders down the chain of command. In the British army troopers memorized calls by putting words to them. The call for "pursue" had the words: "Tis the 'Pursue', make 'em run!"

TRUMPETER
This 19th-century trumpeter of the British Household Cavalry had an elaborate banner attached to his trumpet. Banners were mostly reserved for ceremonial occasions.

WHISTLE
Whistle-blasts could be distinguished, in the din of battle, when shouts might not. Officers in rifle and light infantry regiments, whose men frequently were spread out, used whistles more often than their comrades in line regiments. The cross-belt, with an ammunition pouch at the back and a whistle suspended by a chain on the front, was widely worn by officers of rifle regiments and has been retained for full dress by the British Royal Green Jackets (p. 12).

SMOKE SIGNALS
The need for communication was not confined to formally organized armies. American Indians were skilled at communicating by smoke signals, using a blanket to release smoke in puffs whose meaning could be understood by distant observers. One of the causes of Major General Custer's defeat by Sitting Bull at the Battle of Little Big Horn (1876) was poor contact between advancing columns of cavalry.

DRUMMER
Drummers usually wore a uniform of their regiment's facing colour (the colour of the main uniform's collar and cuffs) with distinctive lace embellishments. This drummer belonged to the British 15th Light Dragoons in 1768.

CIVIL WAR DRUM
Soldiers memorized tunes that regulated life in camp and transmitted orders on the battlefield. If an army was to form up ready to fight, its soldiers would be woken that morning by the long roll of the general call to arms, rather than by the usual reveille (the wake-up call). The drum was used by the infantry, although the bugle, with its better carrying power, became increasingly popular.

Drum skin

Chain prevented whistle being lost

Slider kept drum skin taught

Wood shell

US national symbol

The whistle was stored in this socket attached to the cross-belt when it was not in use

Engineering

MILITARY ENGINEERS helped an army to fight, move, and live. Engineers were particularly concerned with building permanent fortifications and with besieging fortresses. The French engineer Vauban (1633–1707) was responsible for a deep belt of fortifications protecting the borders of France. For many years engineer and artillery officers were better trained than infantry or cavalry officers, to reflect the need to master a range of technical skills. Engineers also constructed field fortifications (including trenches), built or destroyed bridges, made roads and, latterly, railways, and improved the comfort and sanitation of barracks and camps. Some even established reputations as architects.

MEDIEVAL SIEGE
For centuries fortifications and siegecraft were the engineer's chief tasks. The walls of medieval castles were high and thick, making it difficult to get over or through them. Engineers often dug beneath them, making huge underground chambers with roofs held up by wooden props. These chambers, called mines, were packed with inflammable material. When it burnt the props collapsed, and with them the walls of the castle.

TRENCH LOOKOUT
In September 1914 the firepower of modern weapons helped freeze the war of mobility into the stalemate of trench warfare. Elaborate trench systems, with several mutually supporting lines, ran across Belgium and northern France.

Eyepiece

PERISCOPE
Trench warfare encouraged all sorts of ingenuity to enable soldiers to survive in what comfort could be found in trenches and dug-outs. Because snipers (specially trained riflemen) were ready to shoot men who looked over the top of a trench, periscopes were produced which enabled them to observe in safety.

Slope to absorb gun's recoil

BUILDING BRIDGES
Engineers built bridges as well as destroying them. Some bridges rested on floating pontoons: others were suspended on ropes and poles.

Pedal to release cannon

TRAINING
Fortification was a science with rules that engineers had to master. These 19th-century British Royal Engineers trained by building a scale model of fortifications. The broad, low earth walls are designed to resist artillery fire.

EDELSBERG BRIDGE
A retreating army could buy time by destroying bridges, forcing the enemy to build their own. It was a matter of fine judgement as to when bridges should be demolished. Here we see the French attacking Austrians on a bridge near Vienna in 1809, while Austrian engineers try to hack it down to keep the French on the other side.

FRENCH SAPPER
Digging zig-zag trenches towards a besieged fortress was called "sapping", so engineers were often known as sappers. In most armies, infantry regiments contained specialists in field engineering. They were not as widely trained as proper engineers. These men carried axes and wore thick aprons to protect their uniforms. They often sported distinctive beards.

Brass gun barrel

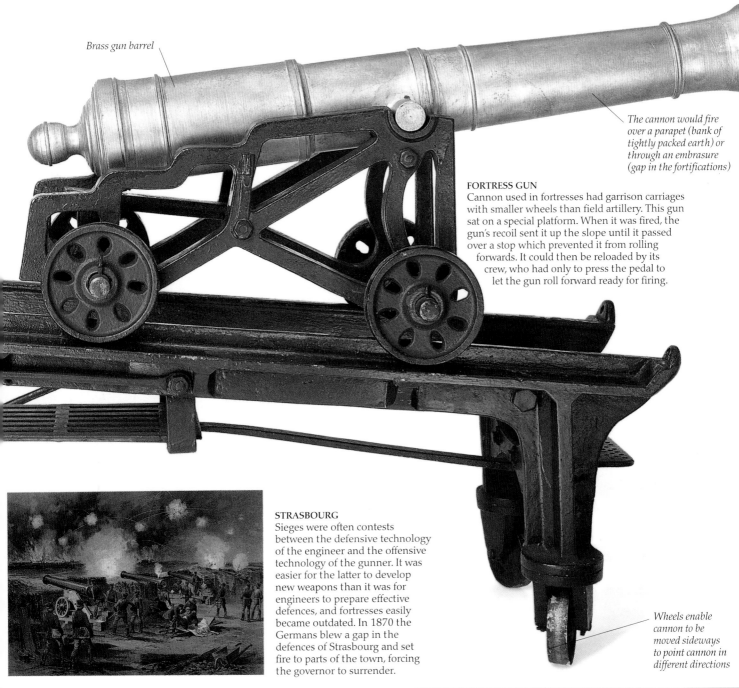

The cannon would fire over a parapet (bank of tightly packed earth) or through an embrasure (gap in the fortifications)

FORTRESS GUN
Cannon used in fortresses had garrison carriages with smaller wheels than field artillery. This gun sat on a special platform. When it was fired, the gun's recoil sent it up the slope until it passed over a stop which prevented it from rolling forwards. It could then be reloaded by its crew, who had only to press the pedal to let the gun roll forward ready for firing.

STRASBOURG
Sieges were often contests between the defensive technology of the engineer and the offensive technology of the gunner. It was easier for the latter to develop new weapons than it was for engineers to prepare effective defences, and fortresses easily became outdated. In 1870 the Germans blew a gap in the defences of Strasbourg and set fire to parts of the town, forcing the governor to surrender.

Wheels enable cannon to be moved sideways to point cannon in different directions

Victory and defeat

ALTHOUGH SOME BATTLES were drawn, with no winner or loser, in most, one side defeated the other. Victory was indicated by the killing or capturing of large numbers of opponents, driving the enemy from the battlefield, or seizing a town or a geographical feature. Sometimes the effects of victory were far-reaching. The Battle of Waterloo (1815) ended the reign of Napoleon and led to a period of stability in Europe. But there was no guarantee that battle would be decisive, and sometimes a long war exhausted both sides. The victor's gains might not justify the human cost of battle. After Waterloo, the British commander, the Duke of Wellington, remarked: "I don't know what it is to lose a battle, but certainly nothing can be more painful than to gain one with the loss of so many of one's friends."

CORONATION OF NAPOLEON
In classical times the laurel symbolized victory, and successful Roman generals who were granted a "triumph" were crowned with laurel and rode through Rome in a chariot. Napoleon wore a crown of laurel at his coronation in 1804 to show that he was a victorious military leader.

Big Elk,
a warrior of the
Omaha tribe

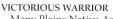

VICTORIOUS WARRIOR
Many Plains Native Americans changed their appearance in some way to show their victories. Big Elk, a warrior of the Omaha tribe, blackened his face to show that he had recently killed an enemy. Victory was also demonstrated by taunting an enemy with a non-lethal blow.

INSTRUMENTS OF VICTORY
Past victories can help win future ones. Soldiers were encouraged to take pride in their regiment's achievements, commemorated in battle honours emblazoned on its colours. These British guardsmen fought fiercely at the Battle of Inkerman (Crimea, 1854) although heavily outnumbered by attacking Russians. Their victory brought a new battle honour.

LOOTING AND PILLAGING
There was often a profit motive in war. Many European noblemen who went on the First Crusade in 1095 were landless younger sons hoping for land in the Middle East. Captured knights were held for ransom, and were released only when their families had paid the money. Common soldiers would pillage if allowed to: here we see a 14th-century army leaving a town it has just sacked, with livestock and other loot. Civilians were the real losers in most campaigns. They were robbed and maltreated by armies that passed by and a long conflict might leave little more than a desert behind it.

PRISONERS AT THE FRONT
Prisoners were sometimes well looked after by the soldiers who captured them but found that treatment worsened in prisoner-of-war camps. These Confederates were captured by Union forces in the US Civil War (1861–1865).

MARQUETRY BOX
A series of international agreements have attempted to ensure that soldiers who surrendered in or after battle were well treated by their captors. Life as a prisoner of war was at best extremely boring, and prisoners often whiled away the hours, and made a little money, by manufacturing trinkets. This straw marquetry box was made by a Napoleonic French prisoner of war in Edinburgh Castle and sold to a local merchant in exchange for provisions.

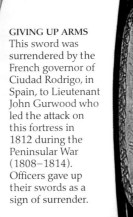

GIVING UP ARMS
This sword was surrendered by the French governor of Ciudad Rodrigo, in Spain, to Lieutenant John Gurwood who led the attack on this fortress in 1812 during the Peninsular War (1808–1814). Officers gave up their swords as a sign of surrender.

Inscription recording the history of the sword

Classical figure of victory

Snake's head popped up when lid was opened

BOOTS
These toy boots were made by a Boer captured by the British during the Boer War (South Africa) of 1899–1902 and sent to a camp in the West Indies. In addition to taking prisoners of war, the British removed Boer women and children from outlying farms to prevent them from helping Boer columns, and housed them in camps where many of them died from disease.

LAST STAND
The last stand of a determined group of soldiers who fight to the death rather than surrender is a popular image for military artists. Here we see a group of British soldiers surrounded by the Boers of Modderfontein in 1901. Such occurrences were relatively rare unless members of the losing side knew that they would be killed if they were taken prisoner.

Inscription shows that sword was made in the Spanish city of Toledo, famous for its high-quality metalwork

Rewards of battle

REGIMENTAL ORDER
In Britain, medals were not generally issued until the 19th century, and this lack of official awards encouraged regiments to produce their own. This order of the 37th was instituted by Sir Eyre Coote of the 37th Regiment in 1774.

MEDALS, ORDERS, AND DECORATIONS are amongst the rewards of battle. Medals are given for gallantry, to commemorate an event, for service in a war, battle or campaign, and for long service or good conduct. Orders of knighthood hark back to medieval knights and have several classes – like a club with members of varying status. They are awarded for a variety of achievements, although some orders are specifically military. Decorations, which are granted for distinguished deeds or bravery, are generally superior to medals but usually lack the different classes found in orders.

DUKE OF WELLINGTON
The Duke of Wellington (1769–1852) commanded the British army that fought the French in Spain and at Waterloo. Here he wears his Gold Cross (a British decoration) as well as the stars of several orders, including the Spanish Order of the Golden Fleece. The Duke, like many senior officers in coalition armies, received numerous foreign orders.

ORDERS
Many orders of knighthood have separate military and civilian divisions, although some are purely military. In full dress uniform, knights wear the star of their order, and the more senior classes of knight wear, in addition, a broad sash over the shoulder. In undress (less formal) uniform, membership of an order will be shown simply by a ribbon worn on the left breast.

BRITAIN
The Most Honourable Order of the Bath traces its origins to 1399. This breast star was worn with a red sash.

FRANCE
The *Légion d'honneur* was established by Napoleon in 1802. It had several classes, for both military and civilian achievement.

THE NETHERLANDS
The Military Order of William was founded by King William I of the Netherlands in 1815, and was awarded for bravery, leadership, and devotion to duty in the presence of the enemy.

MEDALS FOR BRAVERY
Some awards can only be given for bravery in the face of the enemy and are open to servicemen of all ranks. They are often less elaborate than the badges or stars of orders, but are highly prized. A recipient of the Victoria Cross, for example, puts the letters VC, which follow his name, before those for any other awards.

The Victoria Cross, the most coveted British decoration, was instituted in 1856

The New Zealand Cross was instituted by the New Zealand government in 1869

The Medal of Honor, established in 1861, is the US's highest award for bravery

The German Iron Cross was freely awarded for acts of bravery

The Prussian order *Pour le Mérite* became the highest award for gallantry in action

Campaign medals are awarded to individuals for participation in particular campaigns. The different battles the soldier had fought in might be named on bars attached to the ribbon; with some medals, for example the Army Gold Medal, a new medal was awarded after a certain number of bars had been awarded. The recipient's name is usually engraved around the rim of British campaign medals.

The British Waterloo Medal was awarded to all ranks who were present at the battle (1815)

The Queen's South Africa medal was awarded to British soldiers who fought in the Boer War (1899–1902)

The bars on this Military General Service Medal mark actions in Spain in 1812

The Egyptian bronze star awarded to British soldiers in the Egyptian campaigns of 1882–1885

The Army Gold Medal was given to senior British officers who fought in specific battles in 1806–1814

TURKEY
The Turkish Order of Osmanieh was first instituted in 1861–1862 and was awarded to many British officers for their work in Egypt and the Sudan, which were then parts of the Turkish Empire.

RUSSIA
The Order of Saint Anne was founded in Germany in 1735, and was taken over as an Imperial Russian order in 1797. This is an early version of the insignia.

JAPAN
The star of the Japanese Order of the Rising Sun was established in 1875 and has eight classes.

PORTUGAL
The Portuguese Military Order of St Benedict of Aviz began as a religious military order but became secular (non-religious) in 1789. Its badge is a distinctive "cross fleury" (a cross with petal-shaped edges) enamelled in green.

BRITAIN
The Most Exalted Order of the Star of India was instituted by Queen Victoria in 1861.

Sick and wounded

A SURGEON AT WORK
This 16th-century German surgeon is removing a crossbow bolt from a soldier's chest. The French surgeon Ambroise Paré, who lived at this time, was one of the fathers of military medicine. He disagreed with treating wounds with boiling oil, and used a mixture of egg yolk, rose oil, and turpentine instead! With his English contemporaries, Paré did much to improve the status of military doctors.

WOUNDS AND DEATH are commonplace in war, but for hundreds of years many more soldiers died from disease than were killed by the enemy. Ignorance about the bacterial causes of disease long meant that many simple wounds proved fatal, because they were not properly cleaned and dirty instruments were used without being washed between operations. In the US Civil War (1861–1865), for example, 96,000 Union men died in battle but almost twice as many died of disease. Discoveries in medicine and the organization of military medical services improved conditions, but it was not until the Boer War (1899–1902) that a soldier who had an amputation was more likely to survive than to die of gangrene.

RED CROSS ARMBAND
A Swiss banker called Henri Dunant was so shocked when he visited the battlefield of Solferino (Italy) in 1859 that he wrote a book about his experience. This led to the founding of the International Red Cross.

FLORENCE NIGHTINGALE
During the Crimean War (1853–1856) the British base hospital at Scutari in Turkey was in an appalling state, with the sick and wounded lying in corridors, and overflowing lavatories and drains. By November 1854 almost half the patients had died. That month Florence Nightingale (1820–1910) arrived with 38 nurses. Their efforts helped to reduce the death-rate to just 2.3 per cent within six months. There were others who worked to help wounded soldiers, such as Mary Seacole, a Jamaican-born nurse who also ran a lodging house and shop.

SURGEON'S SAW
At Waterloo (1815) the Earl of Uxbridge was hit just below the knee by one of the last cannon-shots fired. This saw was used to amputate his wounded limb. The Earl survived the operation and was fitted with an artificial limb. This earned him the nickname "old peg-leg".

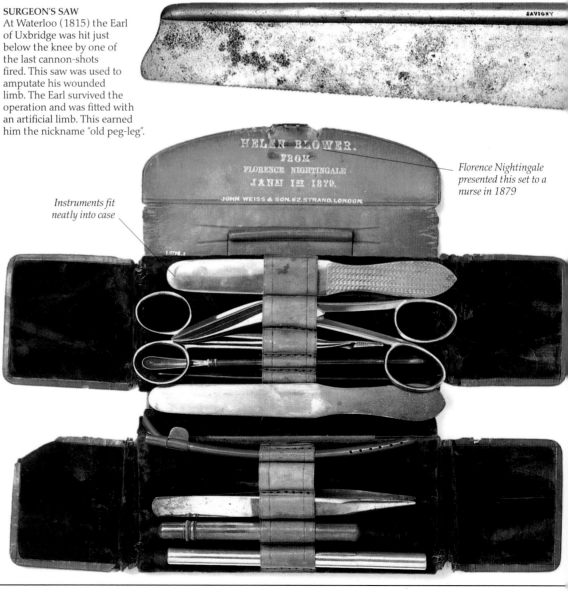

Florence Nightingale presented this set to a nurse in 1879

Instruments fit neatly into case

NURSE'S INSTRUMENTS
Nurses needed instruments to help them dress patients' wounds, cut bandages, and take temperatures. During the Crimean War nursing became an integral part of the armed forces.

THE BATTLE OF INKERMAN
This Crimean battle in the fog cost the British and French over 4,000 casualties and the Russians 12,000. One officer wrote: "I have never witnessed in all my days such a frightful scene of human misery". This picture gives a rosy view of the medical facilities available.

MEDICAL CHEST
Doctors and some nurses equipped themselves with travelling chests containing a wide variety of medicines. This mid-19th-century chest contains stoppered bottles with liquid and powdered medicines which include sedatives and disinfectants. In the drawer there are pharmaceutical scales for weighing out powders, and the needle for a syringe.

Bottles fitted into slots so that they did not break in transit

Ipecacuanha, used to treat coughs and to induce vomiting

Quinine, used to treat fevers

Minim measure, to measure out medicine precisely

Disinfectant

Pills for soothing and curing coughs

Memories of war

COMMEMORATIVE MEDAL
This British medal marks the 200th anniversary of the capture of Quebec by Major General James Wolfe in 1759.

War is remembered in many ways. Some participants thrust dark memories deep into their minds and prefer not to discuss their experiences. It is perhaps true to say that "those that know don't tell, and those that tell don't know". Others recall their exploits with pride, and look back to a time when they felt valued and had comrades upon whom they could rely. Societies often recognize the sacrifice that soldiers have made on their behalf, and commemorate their achievements with war memorials. All too often, though, returning soldiers found themselves neglected; when Frederick the Great of Prussia (1712–1786) saw ex-soldiers begging, he would sometimes say "drive the scum away". Other monarchs did their best for veterans. Louis XIV of France (1638–1715) established the Invalides in Paris as a home for wounded soldiers.

FLOWERS OF THE FIELD
Even after casualties have been removed and nature has healed the scars, battlefields remain poignant places. Lady Hornby, the wife of the British commissioner to Turkey during the Crimean War (1853–1856), pressed flowers from its battlefields. The flower (left) was picked in the "Valley of the Shadow of Death", the scene of the Charge of the Light Brigade (1854), and the flower (below) grew at Inkerman, the scene of another Crimean War battle, which took place in 1854.

Valley of the "Shadow of death."

Inkermann

CAMERAMEN IN DANGER
Newspaper reports from battle-fields provided an independent record of events, and helped civilians to understand the experiences of combatants. These days television reports bring up-to-date battle news.

MAN OF STONE

Edward the Black Prince (1330–1376), eldest son of the British king Edward III, fought in the Hundred Years War (1337–1453) at Crécy and Poitiers, both in France. His nickname originated from his black armour. He was a successful soldier, and was honoured with a burial in Canterbury Cathedral beneath an effigy which shows him in full armour.

WAR MEMORIAL

Britain and its Empire lost a million men in World War I (1914–1918). Their memorials range from tablets in village churches to massive arches and obelisks. This one honours the British Foot Guards.

BURIAL

Prompt and reverend disposal of the dead is crucial for the morale of survivors: no soldier likes to think of lying forgotten on the battlefield. Here we see Japanese dead being buried during the Russo-Japanese War of 1904–1905.

AMERICAN CEMETERY

It was not until World War I that burial of the dead was systematically organized, and policies then adopted by the British and Americans were continued into World War II. The American National Cemetery and Memorial at St Laurent in Normandy has 9,286 graves, including those of 34 pairs of brothers and one father and son.

CRUCIFIX

This crucifix was found on a dead Russian in the Crimea. The image of the crucified Christ is a compelling one for many Christian soldiers, who link their own suffering with his. Soldiers frequently became very attached to religious symbols and goodluck charms, and became deeply depressed if they were accidentally lost.

ICON

The unpredictable nature of war often deepens a soldier's religious faith (though sometimes it does the reverse) or makes him superstitious. Russian soldiers often carried icons (religious pictures) round their necks.

World War II

BETWEEN 1939 AND 1945, 70 million people died in the worst conflict in history – World War II. It was a struggle between the Allies – Britain, Soviet Russia, and the United States (aided by Australia, Canada, France, New Zealand, and others) – against the Axis powers, an alliance of Germany, Italy, and Japan. At first, the Axis powers enjoyed great success, but the Allies eventually triumphed. The turning points were Russia repulsing German forces in Eastern Europe in 1942, the US victory over Japan at the Battle of Midway in the same year, and the Allied invasion of Normandy to liberate German-occupied France in 1944.

BATTLEFIELD AIR POWER

While heavy bombers laid waste to industry, lighter planes became important battlefield weapons. In the early years of the war, the Stuka dive-bomber played key role in Germany's successful *blitzkrieg* ("lightning war") tactics. But by the time of the Allied invasion of Normandy in 1944, the Allies largely controlled the skies. Their fighter-bombers wreaked havoc on German ground forces with bombs, cannons, machine guns, and rockets.

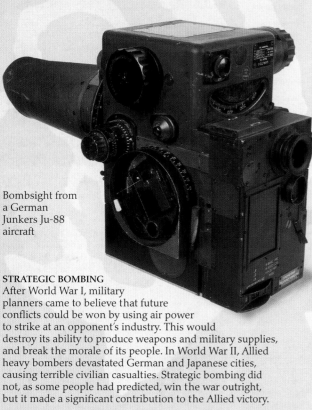

Bombsight from a German Junkers Ju-88 aircraft

British paratroop badge, 1940–1960

Canadian paratroop badge, 1940–1960

STRATEGIC BOMBING

After World War I, military planners came to believe that future conflicts could be won by using air power to strike at an opponent's industry. This would destroy its ability to produce weapons and military supplies, and break the morale of its people. In World War II, Allied heavy bombers devastated German and Japanese cities, causing terrible civilian casualties. Strategic bombing did not, as some people had predicted, win the war outright, but it made a significant contribution to the Allied victory.

AIRBORNE ASSAULTS

Germany's invasion of the Mediterranean island of Crete in 1941 was led by parachute and glider troops. These airborne troops could land behind enemy lines to take the opposition by surprise. American and British airborne forces held the flanks in Normandy in 1944. Later that year, Operation Market Garden was a bold but unsuccessful attempt by Allied parachutists to secure bridges in German-occupied Holland.

RUSIAN FRONT

When the Germans attacked Soviet Russia in 1941 they came close to winning, but the onset of winter left them tantalizingly short of victory. The Germans resumed their advance in 1942, but were brought to a halt at the Russian city of Stalingrad on the River Volga. The Russians gradually pushed the Germans out of Russia, and rolled them back across Eastern Europe to take Berlin, the German capital, in 1945. At the war's end, the Russians controlled most of Eastern Europe, greatly influencing the shape of the postwar world (*see* pp. 66–67).

German troops in Russia, 1941

BATTLE OF THE ATLANTIC

The Allies' ability to keep sea routes open across the Atlantic was key to their success. Merchant ships brought vital supplies from North America to Britain and Soviet Russia, and also US troops to fight in Europe. German U-boat submarine "wolf packs" hunted down and torpedoed supply ships and their naval escorts. Improved Allied warships, better detection equipment, and aircraft support, aided by intelligence from decoded German radio messages, gradually gave the Allies the upper hand.

PROPELLED WEAPONS

TORPEDO

WEAPONS

DEPTH CHARGES

Cigarette cards showing anti-submarine torpedoes and depth charges

Australian troops assault a desert stronghold

WAR IN NORTH AFRICA
In 1939, the Italians held Libya, while Egypt was under British protection. An Italian invasion of Egypt was repelled by the British in the winter of 1940–1941, but Germany then sent its *Afrikakorps* force into the desert war. See-saw advances and retreats followed. The British 8th Army's victory at the Battle of El Alamein in October 1942 finally turned the tide of the North African conflict in the Allies' favour.

Prayer flag carried by a Japanese serviceman

WAR IN THE PACIFIC
At the start of their war against the Allies, the Japanese rampaged across the Pacific region. But defeat to US forces at the naval battle of Midway in June 1942 saw the balance tilt against them. The Americans advanced in the face of fierce defence. The capture of the Marianas Islands brought US bombers within striking range of the Japanese mainland. Dropping atomic bombs on the cities of Hiroshima and Nagasaki in August 1945 finally broke Japanese resolve.

TANK WARFARE
Developed by the British and French in WWI, the tank came into its own in World War II. In 1939–1941, the Germans used it to great effect in its *blitzkrieg* tactics, where it was deployed with infantry, self-propelled artillery, and close air support. The US-made M4 Sherman was the main tank used by the Allies, but it faced formidable opposition in the German Panther and Tiger tanks. By the war's end it was the Russians, with their tough, reliable T-34, who had the advantage in tank warfare. The T-34 remained the mainstay of Russia's armoured divisions in the postwar years.

US-made Sherman tank in British service

An unquiet peace

AFTER THE AXIS DEFEAT IN 1945, the world split into two power-blocs, with the USA and its allies (the West) opposing the Soviet Union and its supporters. This led to the Cold War. Direct conflict between the USA and the Soviet Union did not occur, but there were regional armed clashes as the two superpowers vied to extend their influence on the world. The Cold War ended in the early 1990s with the collapse of the Soviet Union, but hidden ethnic and nationalist tensions resurfaced, resulting in new wars. Religion and competing for natural resources also helped to fuel regional conflicts.

An Israeli tank in the 1967 Yom Kippur War

ARAB-ISRAELI CONFLICTS
The founding of Israel in 1948 provoked an unsuccessful attack by Egypt and other neighbouring Arab states. Further conflicts occurred in 1956, 1967, and 1973. Much of Israel's weaponry was supplied by the West, while the Russians provided arms to the Arab nations. Today, the status of Palestinian Arabs in Israeli-controlled areas is a cause of regional tension, and a key issue in world politics.

Home-made gun used by independence fighters in Kenya against the British, 1950s

WARS OF INDEPENDENCE
In the postwar years, liberation groups fought for independence in some African and Asian countries still ruled by Western colonial powers. Sometimes the rebels, or insurgents, had to resort to making their own weapons. Often the insurgents used ambushes (surprise attacks from hidden positions) and hit-and-run raids against their better-armed opponents.

British SAS badge, bearing the motto "Who dares wins"

SPECIAL FORCES
Special forces units, such as Britain's Special Air Service (SAS), are a key element of the modern army. These elite troops often work far behind enemy lines, carrying out reconnaissance and raids. Although they operate as small groups, their stealth, speed, and teamwork can have a significant impact.

THE RISE OF THE HELICOPTER
Helicopters were in general military use by the 1950s, but it was during the American war in Vietnam (1964–1973) that they really proved their worth. Some helicopters carried troops into battle, and moved vehicles, stores, and ammunition over difficult terrain. Others lifted casualties out of combat zones. When armed with rockets, machine guns, and grenade-launchers, they also functioned as ground-attack aircraft.

US soldiers leap from a Bell UH1-D in the Vietnam War

Russian-made AK-47

Rear sight

Front sight

Folding metal
stock, or handle;
other versions
had a fixed
wooden stock

Trigger

Curved magazine
holds amunition

COLD-WAR KILLER

In 1949, the Russian Army adopted the 30-round
Avtomat Kalashnikova AK-47 automatic rifle.
The Russians also supplied the AK-47 to fellow
Communist states and to forces they supported
in the regional conflicts of the Cold War. Tough,
simple to use, cheap to make, and easy to clean
and maintain, the AK-47 is still in use today. In
all, perhaps 50 million AK-47s have been made.

PORTABLE ANTI-AIRCRAFT MISSILES

The first anti-aircraft missiles were very large
and intended to defend against bombers. The
development of portable missiles changed the
dynamics of the battlefield. Soldiers at last had
an effective weapon against enemy helicopters
and low-flying jets. Insurgents, too, had great
success with these missiles. In the 1980s,
mujahedin fighters in Afghanistan used US-
supplied Stinger missiles against the aircraft
of the occupying Russian forces. They shot
down over 250 aircraft with Stingers before the
Russian Army retreated in 1989. Following the
invasion of Iraq in 2003 by the US-led Coalition
forces, Iraqi insurgents used similar missiles
against Coalition aircraft.

ANTI-AMBUSH VEHICLE

Ambushes have long been a favourite insurgent
tactic. In the early 21st century, insurgents have
made increasing use of Improvised Explosive
Devices (IEDs) and landmines to combine
maximum damage to their opponents with little
risk to themselves. Aware that high casualties
can undermine the public's support for a war,
armies are now equipping themselves with
specially designed vehicles that can withstand
the impact of mines and IEDs.

German soldier with Stinger anti-aircraft missile

Bomb-proof
armoured body

Portable
communications
dish

Dish sends
signals via
satellites in
space

MaxxPro anti-ambush vehicle, widely
used by US-led Coalition forces in Iraq

Electronics and
power pack

BATTLEFIELD COMMUNICATIONS

Information relayed from the battlefield allows
military commanders to build up a picture of
enemy forces and direct their own forces to best
effect. Today, electronic communications systems
aided by computer and satellite technology
create direct, secure links between the combat
zone, headquarters, and even national capitals.
They also keep individual soldiers and units in
touch with one another in the midst of battle.

Find out more

WITH A WEALTH OF INFORMATION available on the Internet, and superb castles, forts, and museums to visit, there are plenty of opportunities to learn more about the lives of soldiers and the experience of battle. Re-enactment groups using replica uniforms and weapons give a sense of living history. Battlefield tours help you to understand key conflicts. To get the most out of your visit or tour, read up about the battle beforehand, and take a tour with an official guide who can explain the terrain to you. Remember that battlefields were not a tourist spectacle to their combatants, many of whom lost their lives there.

Royal Armouries, Leeds, UK

MILITARY MUSEUMS
Museums give a close-up view of weapons, uniforms, and equipment used throughout history, and an overview of the development of military technology. Most museums have education departments whose staff help bring artefacts to life. Notable UK museums include the Imperial War Museum and National Army Museum, London, and the Royal Armouries, Leeds, which also has a base in the Frazie Museum of International History, Lexington, Kentucky, USA.

USEFUL WEBSITES

- For details of UK military museums, visit:
  www.armymuseums.org.uk
- A list of military museums in the US can be found at:
  www.history.army.mil/Museums/links.htm
- The UK's Imperial War Museum has a searchable online database with thousands of images and audio recordings:
  www.iwm.org.uk/
- London's National Army Museum has online exhibitions and collections relating to the history of the British Army:
  www.national-army-museum.ac.uk/
- The website of the Royal Armouries in the UK has video clips and a database of 2,000 thematically arranged images:
  www.royalarmouries.org
- The Australian War Memorial Museum in Canberra has in-depth information about the history of the Australian Army:
  www.awm.gov.au/atwar/
- On All Fronts, a website of the Canadian Film Board, features many film clips relating to World War II:
  www.nfb.ca/ww2/
- The Battlefields Trust's Resource Centre has information on battles in the UK from Roman times onwards:
  www.battlefieldstrust.com/resource-centre/
- America's National Parks Service maintains US battle sites. Select "by topic" on its "Find a Park" search page to locate Civil War and Revolutionary War battlefields:
  www.nps.gov/findapark/index.htm#
- To find the grave of a relative killed in the two world wars, see the Commonwealth War Graves Commission's website:
  www.cwgc.org/
- The American Battle Monuments Commission gives details of war graves for US military personnel:
  www.abmc.gov

Fortifications at Besançon, France

CASTLES AND FORTS
Defences such as castles and forts played a key role in military strategy, and some were the scenes of long, dramatic sieges. Many of these places are open to the public, with displays to help you understand what you are seeing, and perhaps exhibits of arms and armour too. Europe is rich in castles and fortifications. Those designed by France's Marshal Vauban (1633–1707), such as Neuf-Brisach, Besançon, and Le Quesnoy, are great examples of military engineering. In the USA, Fort Ticonderoga, in New York State, and the Alamo, in Texas, are also well worth visiting.

Gettysburg battlefield, Pennsylvania, USA

Military memorabilia

English Civil War re-enactment society

RE-ENACTMENTS
Some military history groups re-enact battles on or near the sites where they were actually fought. There are good annual events at Albuera in Spain (1811) and at Waterloo in Belgium (1815). Other groups do not re-fight battles, but specialize in displays that give a feel for the experience of soldiers in the past.

WAR MEMORIALS
Memorials can be found on battlefields, like those to soldiers who died on the Somme in World War I, or on home soil, such as the US Vietnam Veterans' Memorial in Washington, DC, and the UK Armed Forces Memorial in Staffordshire. Some countries honour unidentified soldiers who died with a tomb to the Unknown Warrior. The UK has one in London's Westminster Abbey; the USA in Arlington National Cemetery, Virginia; and Russia in the Kremlin, Moscow.

BATTLEFIELD TOURS
American battlefields are generally well-maintained. Gettysburg in Pennsylvania (1863), the decisive battle of the American Civil War, is particularly evocative. Sites tend to be less well preserved in the UK, although the 1645 battlefield of Naseby, the key clash of the English Civil War, is being made more accessible to the public. World War I battlefields in France and Belgium are widely visited, especially Ieper (Ypres), the Somme, and Verdun. So too are the beaches of Normandy, France, where Allied invasion forces landed in World War II.

FAMILY CONNECTIONS
Most survivors of World War I have now died, and there are ever-fewer veterans of World War II, but if any of your relatives took part in these wars your family may have kept their letters, photographs, and perhaps medals. Other relatives may have served more recently in the armed forces. They may not want to discuss their combat experiences, but they may be willing to tell you about life in the military.

Kranji War Memorial to Allied soldiers, Singapore

Places to visit

FORT TICONDEROGA, NEW YORK STATE, USA
This fort, which saw action in the Seven Years War (1756–1763) and the American Revolutionary War (1775–1783), has extensive weapons and uniform collections, and also hosts re-enactments.

IMPERIAL WAR MUSEUM, LONDON, UK
Chronicling the history of conflict from World War I to the present day, the museum's vast collections range from tanks and aircraft to photographs and letters.

NATIONAL ARMY MUSEUM, LONDON, UK
Discover the impact the British Army has had on the story of the UK and the wider world.

ROYAL ARMOURIES, LEEDS, UK
A large part of the UK's national collection of arms and armour is housed at the Armouries, with over 8,500 objects on display in five themed galleries.

THE ALAMO, SAN ANTONIO, TEXAS, USA
This former mission and fortress compound was the site of a key battle between the forces of the Republic of Texas and Mexico in 1836.

YORKTOWN BATTLEFIELD, VIRGINIA, USA
Take a tour with a park ranger and find out how American and French forces defeated the British to secure independence for the United States.

WATERLOO, NEAR BRUSSELS, BELGIUM
Tour the site of the final battle of the Napoleonic era. Interpretive material includes audiovisual presentations, films, models, and a wax museum.

Glossary

AMMUNITION Bullets and shells fired by pistols, rifles, machine guns, and artillery.

ANTI-AIRCRAFT MISSILE A ground-to-air missile with an explosive warhead.

Machine gun bullet

ARCHER A person who uses the bow for war, hunting, or target practice.

ARMOUR Protective clothing or coverings worn in combat, usually made of fabric or metal. In the 20th century, the word became a general term for armoured vehicles such as tanks.

ARROW A slender projectile, usually pointed at one end and feathered at the other, that is shot from a bow. Short arrows shot from crossbows are properly called bolts or quarrels.

ARTILLERY Large guns, such as cannons, howitzers, and mortars.

BARRACKS A building or group of buildings that provides permanent accommodation for military personnel.

Artillery gun at the lookout point of Oliver Hill, Western Australia

BATTALION An infantry unit midway in size between a company and a regiment.

BAYONET A bladed weapon that attaches to the muzzle of a firearm. Early bayonets were inserted into the muzzle, but these had the disadvantage of preventing the weapon from being fired when the bayonet was attached.

BILLET Lodgings for a soldier with local inhabitants rather than in an army camp.

BIVOUAC A temporary open-air army camp.

BOW A weapon that uses a tensioned string to shoot an arrow or bolt. Types of bow include the short bows made of horn and sinew used by eastern horse-archers; the medieval wooden longbow; and the medieval crossbow, which had a short bow fixed horizontally to a shaft.

BREECH-LOADER A firearm loaded from the breech (the end of the barrel nearest the user). Breech-loaders could be reloaded and fired more quickly than muzzle-loading weapons.

BROADSWORD A sword with a wide, heavy blade and sharp edges that is designed for slashing and cutting rather than stabbing.

CALIBRE A measure of the inner width of a gun barrel.

CAMOUFLAGE Natural or man-made coverings that are used to disguise and conceal soldiers and their equipment.

CANNON An artillery piece that reaches maximum range when its barrel is at an angle of 45°.

CARBINE A short, smooth-bore or rifled firearm, often used by mounted soldiers.

CARTRIDGE A metal container holding a bullet and gunpowder for use in firearms. Early cartridges were made of paper.

CASE SHOT An iron artillery shell filled with metal balls set in a charge of gunpowder. The shell exploded in the air, showering balls down on to the target. Also called shrapnel.

CASUALTIES Individuals wounded, killed, taken prisoner, or reported missing in battle.

CAVALRY Soldiers who are trained to ride and fight on horseback.

CHARIOT A wheeled, horse-drawn vehicle used in combat.

COLD WAR The military and political tension that existed between Western nations and Soviet Russia and its allies in the aftermath of World War II.

COLOURS The flags carried by infantry regiments. Cavalry regiments traditionally carried smaller banners, known as standards, cornets, or guidons.

COMMISSIONED OFFICER A military leader who is appointed by his or her head of state, and who is part of the recognized officer hierarchy. In most armies the lowest commissioned officer rank is Lieutenant and the highest is Field Marshal.

COMMON SHELL An iron artillery shell filled with gunpowder.

COMPANY For much of history, the smallest infantry unit, typically commanded by a captain. Today, there are smaller units such as platoons and squads.

CUIRASSIER A heavily armoured cavalryman from the 17th to early 19th centuries who wore a metal *cuirass* (breastplate and backplate).

DAGGER A weapon with a short, pointed blade used for stabbing at close quarters.

DRAGOON A 17th-century infantryman who travelled on horseback, but fought mostly on foot. Dragoons eventually became a type of cavalry.

DRILL Repetitive training to promote discipline and instil a set response to orders.

ENGINEER An officer or soldier who constructs fortifications and builds or improves roads, railways, and accommodation. Engineers also try to destroy similar enemy facilities.

FATIGUES Uniform worn by off-duty soldiers.

FLINTLOCK In firearms, a mechanism that ignited the gunpowder charge, using sparks created by striking a flint against a steel plate.

FORTIFICATIONS Defence works that are either permanent, such as castles and forts, or temporary, such as trenches and bunkers.

GRAPESHOT A container of musket balls fired from a cannon. It split up as it left the cannon, scattering the balls at approaching troops. Grapeshot caused terrible casualties when used at close range. Also called canister.

Turkish Tufenjieff grenade

GREAVES Metal shinguards worn by many warriors in ancient times.

GRENADE In the 17th and 18th centuries, gunpowder-filled ceramic or iron globes thrown by individual soldiers. The 20th century saw the introduction of rifle-grenades, which could be fired from rifles.

GRENADIER Originally, an infantryman who was trained to throw grenades. The term was later used more generally to refer to elite troops.

GUNPOWDER An explosive mixture of sulphur, saltpetre, and charcoal used to propel bullets and shells from firearms and artillery.

HALBERD A long-handled weapon topped by an axe-blade and a sharp point. Halberds were carried by infantry sergeants in the 18th century.

HELIOGRAPH A tripod-mounted mirror that was used to send signals as flashes of reflected sunlight.

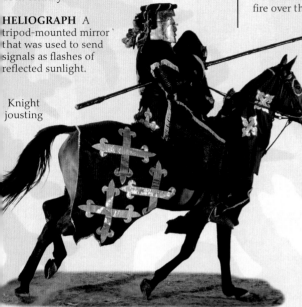

Knight jousting

HOWITZER An artillery piece for firing shells at high angles (more than 45°). Howitzers tend to have longer barrels than mortars.

HUSSAR A type of light cavalryman mounted on a fast horse. Hussars typically took part in skirmishing and reconnaissance.

INFANTRY Soldiers who fight on foot. Infantry traditionally formed the bulk of most armies.

INSURGENT A fighter, typically not part of a conventional military force, who wages war against either the state or an occupying army.

KNIGHT A mounted and armoured warrior, usually of noble birth. Knights dominated warfare for much of the Middle Ages.

LANCE A weapon used in mounted combat, especially by knights, with a long wooden shaft and a sharp metal head.

LEGIONARY A soldier of ancient Rome.

LIGHT TROOPS Infantry and cavalry trained to move quickly and use light weapons.

LIMBER A small, horse-drawn carriage for towing a cannon. The limber carried tools and ammunition for the cannon.

LOGISTICS The practical art of moving bodies of troops and keeping them supplied.

MACE A hand-held weapon with a heavy metal head, often with metal spikes or flanges.

MACHINE-GUN A rapid-fire weapon, often of rifle calibre, with its ammunition generally contained in a fabric belt or metal magazine.

MAGAZINE The ammunition container attached to a rifle or machine gun.

MATCHLOCK A primitive form of firearm ignition, in which a smouldering cord was used to ignite the weapon's gunpowder charge.

MORTAR A short-barrelled artillery piece used to launch explosive projectiles, properly called "bombs", at a high angle (more than 45°). Mortars were often used in sieges, because they could fire over the top of fortifications and defences.

MUSKET A smooth-bore, muzzle-loading firearm that preceded the rifle.

MUZZLE-LOADER A firearm that is loaded by inserting the charge and projectile into its muzzle (the end farthest from the user).

NCO (non-commissioned officer) A soldier who ranks between a private (ordinary soldier) and a commissioned officer. NCOs are appointed from within the army, rather than by the state. Corporals and sergeants are NCOs.

PHALANX A closely packed body of infantry. It was the formation used by hoplite warriors in ancient Greece.

PIKE An infantry weapon consisting of an extremely long wooden shaft with a sharp iron tip.

PISTOL A firearm that can be used one-handed. Pistols were traditionally carried by cavalry and officers, and sometimes as personal protection by soldiers (such as military policemen) whose main role was not direct combat.

American Civil War sabre

POLEAXE A weapon consisting of an axe-head mounted on a long shaft.

PRISONERS OF WAR Soldiers captured in battle or as a result of formal surrender.

QUADRANT A device for measuring the firing angle of an artillery piece to calculate how far a shot would go.

RANK An soldier's status in the military hierarchy, usually used as a prefix to his or her name, as in Major Smith.

RAPIER A thin-bladed sword used for thrusting and stabbing.

RECONNAISSANCE Scouting and patrolling to gather details of terrain or of the enemy's strength, location, and behaviour.

REGIMENT A military unit made up of several battalions, often with a geographical title (Middlesex Regiment) or number (22nd Regiment). The groupings above the regiment are, in increasing size: brigade, division, corps, army, and army group.

RIFLE A firearm with spiral grooves (rifling) on the inside of its barrel. The grooves spin the bullet or shell in flight, increasing its stability and accuracy.

ROUND SHOT Artillery ammunition consisting of solid balls made at first from stone, and later from iron.

SABRE A type of heavy sword with a curving blade, used mainly by cavalry.

SAMURAI Members of a warrior class that enjoyed elite status in medieval Japanese society. In many ways, the samurai were the Japanese equivalent of European knights.

British colonel's rank slide, worn over the epaulette

SAPPER Another word for an army engineer. The word comes from the practice of "sapping", when engineers would dig zig-zag trenches towards a besieged fortress.

SIEGE The practice of blockading a city, town, or fortress by military forces in order to capture it. If the attackers could not break through the fortifications, a lack of food and water would often force the defenders to surrender.

SKIRMISHING Harassing the enemy by engaging them in short battles with small groups of mobile troops.

SMOOTH-BORE BARREL A gun barrel with a smooth inner surface (*see* Rifle).

SPEAR A long shaft with a sharply pointed end, used for throwing or thrusting. Throwing spears are often called javelins.

SPECIAL FORCES Elite troops who carry out high-risk missions behind enemy lines.

STRATEGIC BOMBING The use of heavy bombing by aircraft to destroy an enemy's industrial and military capacity, and to undermine the morale of its people.

SWORD A long-bladed weapon for cutting, slashing, or stabbing.

TACTICS The art of fighting battles and military engagements.

TANK A heavily armored combat vehicle that moves on continuous tracks, usually armed with cannon and machine guns.

TRENCH A man-made ditch with reinforced sides, used for protection. Trenches could be continuous, as in World War I, or one- or two-man "foxholes".

Automatic Colt 1911 A1 Pistol

WAR HAMMER A handled weapon with a hammer-head on one side and a sharp spike on the other.

Index

Acknowledgements

Dorling Kindersley would like to thank: For their help with photography and information: 95th Rifles and Re-enactment Living History Unit (Les Handscombe, Martin Handscombe, Dennis Wraight, Nick McMillan); the Army Museums Ogilby Trust; Angels and Bermans (film costumiers); the British Museum (Nick Nicholls of the photographic service); Mark Dennis; David Edge (Histrionix Ltd) and Mark Churms, Paul Ellis, Pierre-de-Hugo, Anthony Perkins, Chris Seidler, and Ian Smith; Freddie Edge; the Trustees of the Florence Nightingale Museum (and Timothy Bonham-Carter); Stephen Naegel; the Museum of Artillery in the Rotunda, (Stan Walter); the Royal Green Jackets Museum (Major R.D. Cassidy); the Trustees of the National Museum of Scotland (Scottish United Services Museum); the Sulgrave Manor Board, Northamptonshire; the Trustees of the Wallace Collection, London. For additional special photography: Peter Chadwick: pp. 30-31, 33, 49, 50. For design and editorial help: Mark Haygarth, Joseph Hoyle, Susan St. Louis, Gin von Noorden. For the index: Hilary Bird.

For this edition, the publisher would also like to thank: author Richard Holmes for assisting with the updates; Lisa Stock for editorial assistance; David Ekholm-JAlbum, Sunita Gahir, Susan St Louis, Steve Setford, Lisa Stock, and Bulent Yusuf for the clipart; Sue Nicholson and Edward Kinsey for the wallchart; Monica Byles and Stewart J Wild for proofreading.

Picture credits
The publisher would like to thank the following for their kind permission to reproduce their photographs:

(Key: a-above; b-below/bottom; c-centre; f-far; l-left; r-right; t-top)
Ancient Art and Architecture Collection: 14ar, 37ar, 56al. **akg-images:** 64bc. **Alamy Images:** Jon Arnold Images Ltd 68cr; Dennis MacDonald 68-69b. **The Board of Trustees of the Armouries:** Bibliothèque des arts décoratifs: 33cr, 43ar; Bibliothèque nationale, Paris: 36bl; British Library: 45br, 49al, 54ar; Jean-Loup Charmet: 32al, 32cr, 32cl, 33bcr, 37bcl, 46ar; Imperial War Museum, London (I Want you for the U.S. Army by James Montgomery Flagg, 1917): 68tr. **Bridgeman Art Library:** John Spink Fine Watercolours, London: 9br; Private Collection: 38br. **Corbis:** Bettmann 66b; Henri Bureau / Sygma 66tr; Randy Faris 64-65, 66-67, 68-69, 70-71(background). **DK Images:** The Board of Trustees of the Armouries 67t; Gettysburg National Military Park, PA 71crb; Imperial War Museum 64cl, 70crb, 71tr; Judith Miller / Wallis and Wallis 69tr; Museum of the Regiments, Calgary 64-65b; Rough Guides 69c; Lieutenant Commander W.M. Thornton MBE RD RNR 64cr. **E.T. Archive:** 16ar, 20cl, 21al, 24acl, 26bl, 36br, 44al, 52bl, 53al, 56br, 57bc; Bibliothèque nationale, Paris: 7cl; Musée Malmaison: 49ar; Museum der Stadt, Wien: 55al; Parker Gallery: 26br. **Fitzwilliam Museum, University of Cambridge:** 16cr. **Michael Holford:** 7ar, 15al. **Hulton-Deutsch Collection:** 8al, 26bcr, 27bl, 28br, 30al, 34br, 34bl, 56ar. **Imperial War Museum:** 66ca. **Mansell Collection:** 20cr, 36al, 36ar, 42bc. **Mary Evans Picture Library:** 12al, 13cr, 14cr, 15ar, 18br, 20bc, 25ar, 29cr, 31ar, 39acr, 41al, 42ar, 44cl, 46al, 50cl, 52ar, 54bc, 55bl, 60al, 60cl, 61al, 62bl, 63ar; Explorer Archives: 20al. **Musée de l'Armée, Paris:** 18al, 18-19a, 27br, 44ar. © **National Army Museum, London** - photograph supplied by Bridgeman Art Library: 16br. **PA Photos:** DPA 67cra; Haraz N. Ghanbari / AP 67clb. **Peter Newark's Military Pictures:** 10al, 19cr, 31br, 35al, 43al, 46bl, 51acl, 51bcr, 51bl, 52ac, 54acl, 56bl, 57tc, 58ar, 63tc. **Range / Bettmann:** 50al. **Robert Harding Picture Library:** 63cr; Musée de l'Armée: 55ar. **Trustees of the Royal Hussars Museum:** 25bcr. **Shutterstock:** Ovidiu Lordachi 67br; Stephen Mulcahey 69tl.

Science Museum / Science & Society Picture Library: 25al. **Mr. A.D. Theobald, courtesy of the Royal Signals Museum:** 52al. **TopFoto.co.uk:** 64tr, 65tr. **Jo Walton** 66cl.

Wallchart
The Bridgeman Art Library: John Spink Fine Watercolours, London, UK cl; **DK Images:** The 95th Rifles and Re-enactment Living History Unit cra, crb (trumpet); Gettysburg National Military Park, PA bl; Royal Green Jackets Museum, Winchester bc, clb (Spanish rapier), cr (sketch and telescope), fcra; Wallace Collection, London fclb (war hammer and mace).

All other images © Dorling Kindersley
For further information see:
www.dkimages.com